NATURAL**DISASTERS**
THE TERRIFYING FORCES OF NATURE

NATURAL**DISASTERS**
THE TERRIFYING FORCES OF NATURE

Karen Farrington

GRAMERCY

This 1999 edition is published by Gramercy Books™,
a division of Random House Value Publishing, Inc.,
201 East 50th Street, New York, New York, 10022.
by arrangement with PRC Publishing Ltd, London.

Gramercy Books™ and design are registered trademarks of
Random House Value Publishing, Inc.
Random House
New York • Toronto • London • Sydney • Auckland
http://www.randomhouse.com/

Printed and bound in China
A CIP catalogue record for this book is available from the Library of Congress.

ISBN 0-517-16144-3

8 7 6 5 4 3 2 1

contents

INTRODUCTION

Right: Tornadoes such as this are responsible for widespread destruction throughout the area known as "Tornado Alley" in the southern states of the US.

Human existence has always been fragile, clinging to the surface of an unstable planet. Below us, molten rock seethes, and the tectonic plates that make up the thin barrier between us and this fiery magma are in a state of constant friction, threatening to topple buildings or cause vast tsunami waves that can devastate coastal regions at any time. Above us, the skies churn with violence—hurricanes and tornadoes can wreak destruction with unimaginable power and sudden downpours can drown prosperous towns, flood waters rushing through the streets at a furious pace.

High ground is not safe either. The rocks, mud, and snow that adheres to the steep slopes often breaks loose, sending landslides and avalanches racing down mountains to consume anything in their path.

The science of prediction now gives occasional warnings of these dreadful occurances, perhaps allowing a little time for evacuation. But there is still no averting the power of nature and very little that we can do to minimize the damage.

EARTH**QUAKES**

Right: Soldiers search through earthquake rubble. Despite many years of research into making buildings earthquake proof, the only real test of their power to withstand a tremor comes when they are actually hit by a quake. Many fail to live up to their architects' expectations.

When fish jump from the water, when pigs chew off their tails, when cats begin a frenzied four-paw dance, it can mean only one thing. An earthquake is imminent. Those observing such strange animal behavior would do well to heed the warning displayed by those helplessly driven creatures. The finely attuned sensory perceptions of animals give them a valuable advantage over us humans. Although years of effort and investment have gone into the business of predicting earthquakes, forewarning of impending disasters is far from foolproof.

On February 4, 1975, the Chinese authorities acted swiftly when they noticed bizarre antics among the animal population and registered a series of minor tremors in the earth's crust increasing in frequency and velocity. Residents in the southern Liaoning province were told to quit their homes and head for the open countryside. Within hours, a quake had struck which destroyed two cities. The death toll was a remarkably modest 300 in a region where the population exceeded 90,000.

However, just 16 months later there was a cataclysmic catastrophe when the early warning system somehow failed. In the early hours of July 28, 1976, Tangshan city was all but destroyed by a substantial earth tremor, which was followed by an aftershock of similar force just 36 hours later. The death toll was a staggering 242,000.

International giants Russia, the United States, China, and Japan are the world leaders in earthquake prediction, seeking evidence of forthcoming natural disasters in the onset of low-velocity tremors, fluctuating water levels, changes in the magnetic field, and—with the help of satellite— bulging in the earth's surface, as well as inexplicable animal exploits. They are rightly buoyed by their successes. However, the apparently random behavior of planet earth and her outbursts of stress and tension many times greater than any nuclear explosion makes their task a monumental one. The technological prowess of humanity comes to nothing in the face of these disasters, when nature proves once again that she still wields greater power than we could imagine.

The world has shuddered at the beckoning of earthquakes since time began. The ancient Greeks fancied they were caused by winds whistling beneath the earth's surface until rival philosophers deemed that subterranean blazes were to blame. In India, it was long held that the giant water buffalo on whose back the world was perched was scratching himself. The Rumanians, believing the earth stood upon the three pillars of faith, hope, and charity, blamed human erring for undermining those supports. Other mystical, magical explanations crop up in different world cultures. Christianity long claimed it was an act of retribution against sinners by God. This must have come as a shock to the 40 worshippers doing their Christian duty in church at San Juan Capistrano who were killed on December 8, 1812, during an earthquake!

Right: For those trapped inside devastated buildings such as these, relief may take a long while coming as rescue workers will be hampered by the effects of the earthquake such as loss of electricity and communications. Vital equipment may also be difficult to move into the stricken area due to damage to transport routes.

In fact there are three reasons that earthquakes occur. The most crucial is the movement of the plates that make up the world's crust. Sometimes they grind against one another. Occasionally one slides beneath another. The result is an earthquake, which may be minor or, quite literally, earth shattering. However, despite popular belief, there's no "opening of the earth" as depicted in some novels and films. If that occurred there would be no friction and consequently no tremors.

Some areas are more prone to earthquakes than others because they are sited where two plates abut one another. The most famous of these "faults" is the so-called "Ring of Fire," which follows a 38,600 kilometer (24,000 mile) route that effectively borders the Pacific Ocean. Another fault scythes through southern Europe. However, earthquakes are not restricted to the rupture of the plate edges. Some occur in the middle of plates like those that shook Madrid, Missouri, in 1811 and 1812—these tremors were powerful enough to redirect the path of the Mississippi River.

The point at which the tension between the earth's plates is greatest, causing the earthquake to erupt, may be miles inside the earth. This is the focus of the earthquake. Shallow earthquakes are those with a focus up to 70 kilometers (44 miles) beneath the earth's surface. Intermediate earthquakes have a focus between 70 and 300 kilometers (44 and 188 miles) down, while deep earthquakes go even further towards the core. The deepest on record was 720 kilometers (447 miles) down, below the Flores Sea in Indonesia on June 29, 1934. The region on the world's surface corresponding to the focus is called the epicenter.

The other two causes of earthquakes are volcanoes—although these tend to cause only minor rumblings—and man. Human endeavors such as making dams or reservoirs, detonating explosions, or mine workings have sparked earth movement.

Earthquake shock waves come in six discernible categories. Briefly, there are pressure waves, or P-waves, which follow the direction of the tremor, while shear waves or S-waves travel up and down. There are also surface seismic waves L-waves—taking their initial from the British geophysicist Augustus Love—and R-waves, named in honor of British physicist John Rayleigh.

The disaster of a major earthquake has many facets. Most immediately there is nowhere to run, no safe place to hide. Undulating earth causes buildings to destabilize and crumble in the space of a few short seconds and a thunderous roar that accompanies a violent shaking motion is equally terrifying. The ancient oriental manner of building using bamboo and paper is most suited to earthquake regions as it is lightweight, so inhabitants are not injured by it, and it is quick to replace. Alas, modern living demands more than bamboo and paper constructions can offer and

Above: An elementary school that has been hit by an earthquake.

Right: A building damaged by the Kobe earthquake that hit Japan on January 17, 1995. The whole area, which was completely unprepared for earthquakes, was destroyed.

the usual array of building materials prevail, including bricks, concrete, steel girders and so forth. The danger these heavily constructed homes and office blocks present to those within during an earthquake is instantly apparent. Those who do not perish instantly as buildings collapse on top of them may be buried for days under the rubble. Engineers are developing new methods to combat the effects of earthquakes, including the use of "shock absorbers" in the foundations in the form of rubber cushioning. The Japanese are experimenting with the building of large swaying pendulums into tall buildings to counteract the swing created in an earthquake.

Soil is liquefied in an earthquake, taking on the properties of quicksand. Landfill sites are therefore particularly vulnerable during an earthquake—buildings on them will tumble and sink.

Power lines are brought down—which may prove crucial to the efficiency of rescue work in the hours of darkness—and highways are destroyed, hampering the journey of emergency vehicles. Telephone landlines are also likely to be out of action.

Sewers may be exposed or ruptured, which in turn could affect the safety of the water supply, increasing the threat of disease.

The initial, devastating tremor may be followed by numerous aftershocks. Characteristically these are less severe but still may cause damage to destabilized buildings.

An earthquake may unleash a landslide, causing further havoc, or brew a tidal wave. These mighty waves, perhaps 30 meters (100 feet) high and traveling at enormous speed, have nothing to do with tides and are generally now referred to by their Japanese name, *tsunamis*. At sea a tsunami appears to be nothing greater than an extraordinary swell, but when the wave approaches the shore it can build up to an awesome size and wreak havoc. As land dwellers have discovered to their cost, tsunamis may occur following an ocean bed earthquake that few have registered. In 1896, the Japanese town of Sanriku with a population of some 20,000 was wiped out by this kind of wave.

Fires are often caused by the disruption to electricity, gas, or oil supplies and major machinery. Following a catastrophe, fire fighters, water, and equipment are invariably scarce and, accordingly, small blazes often escalate.

Those caught in the aftermath of an earthquake are advised to use a battery operated or car radio to listen for news. However, they should not attempt to drive anywhere as those roads that are not blocked should be left free for emergency vehicles.

It is important that weakened homes are evacuated, and strong footwear, to protect feet from glass shards and debris, as well as warm clothing should be taken. However, if the building is robust, it is better to

Right: Although the ripping of the earth often seen in movies is extremely rare, earthquakes can cause tension cracks like this in the ground.

stay inside to avoid danger from tumbling debris in the streets. Downed power lines or objects near them must never be touched. Following an earthquake there are often reports of strange lights and fiery glows, which may be caused by fires or static electricity.

An earthquake is measured by a seismograph which, at its most basic, has a suspended weight that remains stationary when the environment around it shakes. The weight is used as a marker against a rotating drum to get a pattern of the earth's movement. Since the first seismograph was invented at the end of the 19th century the instrument has been honed and today uses electromagnetic as well as visual methods of record.

Two scales most familiarly record the velocity of earthquakes around the world. The logarithmic Richter scale invented by American Charles Richter in 1935 gives a measurement between 0 and 9. Bear in mind its mode of operation and that an earthquake that records six on the Richter scale is 10 times more powerful than one which measures five and 100 times more powerful than the one which notches up four.

The second scale is that produced by Italian seismologist Giuseppe Mercalli in 1902. This is denoted in Roman numerals which range from an insignificant I through to a ferocious XII. It measures the intensity of shaking and has been modified for modern use.

Despite leaps in technology it still remains impossible to tell when an earthquake is going to strike. Observations made during the 20th century lead seismologists to assume that there will be one great earthquake in the world every year, measuring eight or above on the Richter Scale. There's the potential for 18 major earthquakes a year measuring from seven up to eight on the scale and 120 in the range of six. Moderate earthquakes, measuring between five and six on the Richter Scale, number 800 on average each year while earthquakes registering above four but below five occur 6,200 annually. Very minor earthquakes, measuring less than three on the Richter scale, happen at the rate of about 9,000 per day.

Thankfully not all earthquakes are the cause of massive loss of life. That only happens when the earthquake occurs in a region of high population. Two of the largest recorded in modern times — one 320 kilometers (200 miles) off the coast of Columbia on 31 January 1906 and another off the coast of Honshu, Japan, on 2 March 1933 — both reached 8.9 on the Richter Scale. But only the face of the seabed was dramatically altered as both occurred under the oceans.

VOLC**A**NOES

Right: The eruption of a volcano is an awesome, terrifyingly beautiful sight for those lucky enough to be out of danger.

The trigger for an earthquake is sometimes a volcano, a grumbling mountain built around a natural chimney that occasionally spews rocks, lava, or gases from inner earth. Volcanoes are, like earthquakes, among nature's most terrible spectacles. The sight of an erupting volcano inspires awe and fear in equal measure.

Usually, volcanoes are conical in shape although some defy the norm and are larger with more gently sloping sides. These are known as shield volcanoes, the largest of which is Mauna Loa on Hawaii—a staggering 4,170 meters (13,680 feet) high, 120 kilometers (75 miles) long, and 50 kilometers (31 miles) wide. Its crater covers an area of six and a half kilometers (four miles).

A volcano occurs when molten rock (called magma) below the earth's surface comes under pressure from gas which forces it through a vent in the earth, pushing the land upwards. Some volcanoes, like Stromboli in Italy and Kilauea in Hawaii, are perpetually active, while others are entirely dormant. It is the behavior of erratic volcanoes outside these two camps that can surprise us. Those violent eruptions, which occur after years of quiet contemplation, generally lead to the greatest natural disasters. That eruption may be over in a few moments or could last for days, months, or even years before subsiding—the volcano Paricutin in Mexico erupted for nine years before it was quiet again.

Given the scale of death and destruction that volcanoes have caused since ancient times it is a wonder that anyone would choose to live in their shadow. Yet colonies spring up around the bases of the belching giants precisely because of their previous volcanic activity. In the long term, the mineral products of volcanoes make the surrounding areas abnormally fertile as the riches that abound inside the earth are now laid bare on its surface. The heat in natural springs can also be tapped and places as diverse as California, New Zealand, and Iceland take advantage of nature's water heating system for showers, central heating, and the creation of electricity. Volcanoes are also things of great beauty—their scenic value gives an area great appeal.

An abundance of myths have grown up around volcanoes, which is hardly surprising. The sight of one of these mountains ferociously spewing flame would easily lead one to suppose that it is powered by supernatural forces. A succession of volcanic eruptions in the Aegean Sea in around 1600BC was blamed for the obliteration of Atlantis and its sophisticated population. Fallout from the same volcano is thought to be responsible for the bombardment suffered by Jason and the Argonauts, which, at the time, was attributed to the vindictive action of a giant. The fable claims that Medea overcame the monster, making his blood flow "like molten lead." This was, in reality, surely lava. It was probably a tsunami triggered at the same time that wiped out Knossus, the capital of

Right: Hot lava is not the only hazard associated with volcanoes. This town has been inundated with a blanket of volcanic mud. While in the short-term this causes massive destruction, in years to come it will make the soil of the area particularly fertile.

Far Right: In the background, Mt Unzen in Japan continues to erupt while a survivor examines the wreckage of a home destoyed by the mud-flow.

Crete, and brought the peaceful Minoan civilization to its doom. Volcanoes were later the domain of Greek and Roman fire gods at work with hammer and anvil in a forge who would occasionally visit their frustrations on the population.

In Nicaragua, it became customary to sacrifice a virgin by throwing her into the lava lake at Masaya to appease the volcano. In nearby El Salvador the sacrifice was of a child, bound hand and foot. Many cultures across the globe hold volcanoes to be sacred, entirely because of their immense power.

Volcanoes also have an uncanny resemblance to the Old Testament descriptions of hell and it was perhaps an eruption that caused the destruction of Sodom and Gomorrah.

But just what does happen when volcanoes blow? Volcanoes are not uniform in their outbursts. In the imagination, an exploding volcano sends streams of glowing lava down its sides, slowly but surely engulfing everything in its path. This is typical of the effusive volcanoes found around Hawaii which are known as Basaltic. Devastating they may be, but the nature of the eruption gives people in the surrounding areas plenty of time to evacuate safely.

Other volcanoes blow with a bang and these are termed Andesitic. When they occur there may not be time to flee the molten rock, landslides, ash clouds, and downpour of boulders that follow. When there is a sudden and violent explosion of steam, gas, pumice, and ash which moves at speed, the resulting ash flow and cloud plume are together known as a *nuée ardente*, French for glowing cloud. There is little hope of escape for those in the vicinity.

Despite all the study that has taken place into volcanoes it remains difficult to know just how individuals are going to behave.

Right: An aerial view of Unzen, a volcano in northern Kyushu, shows the path of a pyroclastic flow expelled by the volcano. It wiped out or flooded a large section of Shimabara, a town on the coast below.

Lava flows shift at between a few centimeters to several kilometers per hour, depending on their temperature (between 550 degrees and 1400 degrees centigrade), the steepness of the slope, and the amount of the mineral silica (which is abundant in the earth's crust) they contain. One extraordinarily swift flow traveling at a top speed of about 110 kilometers per hour (70 miles per hour) claimed the lives of about 300 people when it occurred at Mt Nyiragongo in Zaire. Usually the greatest danger the lava presents is to buildings, as it will bury and burn anything in its path. And it sometimes dams rivers or melts ice, causing flooding. People have attempted to counter it by building barriers or by using explosions to divert its path or by spraying it with cooling water.

More hazardous are the fiery "pyroclastic" flows which come from explosive rather than effusive volcanoes, and are turbulent with gas, rock fragments, and intense heat. These travel at great speed. "Lahars" are similar to pyroclastic flows but contain more water, frequently precipitating mudslides. Pyroclastic surges are lower in density and contain more gas but are equally dangerous, with the power to asphyxiate.

The material that spurts forth from explosively erupting volcanoes is known as "tephra." Biggest among the family of tephra are blocks and bombs, which can be as mighty as 30 tons. Blasted out of the volcano in a powerful eruption of gas they may land many miles from the volcano and clearly present a shockingly unexpected danger.

Tephra also includes "lapilli," detritus that measures up to 6.5 centimeters (2.5 inches), as well as grain-sized ash that sometimes combines with water in the atmosphere to produce larger particles. To combat the harmful effects of tephra, housebuilders in volcanic areas often include steep slopes in the pitch of their roofs. This avoids the hazard of tephra collecting on flat roofs and causing a cave-in. Ash is something of a wild card and may be carried vast distances, depending on wind speed and weather. People caught up in ash clouds—which are not only choking but may contain harmful gases—should go out only wearing masks or wet cloths over their mouths.

Airborne ash obviously reduces visibility and this increases the likelihood of road crashes. However, its dangers do not end there: it will also affect TV, telephone lines, electricity cables, and may clog water supplies, machinery, nuclear power plants, storm sewers, and sewerage systems. In 1982, the engines of two jet aircraft failed, with consequent loss of life, due to the ash emitted by the Galunggung Volcano in West Java. Ash can also scorch vegetation and cause lasting famine in the aftermath of an eruption. In addition to these hazards, it seems certain that volcanic ash influences world weather patterns.

Volcanic gases are the unseen hazard and have their own sinister part to play in such natural disasters. The gases are an unsavory mixture of

Right: Mud and rock from a pyroclastic flow expelled by the Unzen volcano flooded this residential area of Shimabara.

Below: The smoking summit of Mt Unzen, Japan.

carbon dioxide, sulfur dioxide, hydrochloric acid, hydrogen fluoride, methane, hydrogen, and carbon monoxide, among others. Although volcanic gases have a tendency to cling to tephra they are generally soon dispersed into the atmosphere. Tragically, however, that doesn't always happen—the plight of those living around Lake Nyos in Cameroon teaches a valuable lesson. The inhabitants may have been aware that the lake was sitting inside the crater of a volcano. They might yet have known that the volcano still belched forth deadly gases into the waters of the lake. Until August 21, 1986, however, those gases lurked at the bottom of the lake while harmless water covered the top.

For reasons which are still not clear, the noxious gases broke the surface of the lake, surged upwards like an invisible bubble which then rolled down the mountainside at a speed of some 50 kilometers per hour (30 miles per hour) suffocating everything in its path. It survived for 25 kilometers (15 miles) before breaking up into the atmosphere. The result was that while cattle grazing near the lake were unaffected, livestock and people further down were left dead. Such was the bizarre nature of the disaster that patients on the first floor of a hospital ten kilometers (six miles) from the lake survived while those on the ground floor were killed. The lucky ones lost consciousness in the absence of oxygen but awoke hours later when the danger had passed. The final death toll was 1,700.

These gases are also the cause of acid rain—harmful to skin, vegetation and, water supplies and may be responsible for climate changes.

Volcanoes can erupt without causing massive loss of life. In fact, one of the greatest explosions of the 20th century appeared to have not claimed a single casualty. It occurred when Mount Bezimiannyi on the remote Kamchatka Peninsula in Russia defied experts who considered it extinct by blowing out about 2,400 million tons of rubble from its chimney in 1955. Fortunately no one lived within miles of the catastrophe.

An extinct volcano will be subject to weather erosion and collapse until it is finally indistinguishable from the rest of the landscape.

AVALANCHES

Above: Fortunately most avalanches occur in inacessible places. But when one hits a mountain village or ski resort the results can be tragic.

Right: These lucky mountaineers escaped the avalanche that falls behind them although it may have been their movements across the snow that caused the slippage.

Avalanches are the catastrophic snow slips that claim scores of lives each year. The most likely cause of an avalanche is the skier, snowboarder, or climber whose movements across a snow-loaded slope unwittingly destabilizes the snow, which then engulfs them. It's not a case of being in the wrong place at the wrong time, the avalanche simply would not have occurred had the unlucky sportsperson not ventured there in the first place. It is no coincidence that those who use the snow for recreations comprise the vast majority of casualties.

This is a comparatively new finding although one could say that avalanches are as old as the hills they crash down. Comprehending this natural phenomena is a relatively recent scientific advance. After all, the vast majority occur naturally in the uninhabited and hostile Himalayas and it is only when avalanches paralyze the more accessible peaks, like the Alps in Europe and the Rockies in America, that they pose a threat. With new scientific knowledge it is now clear why so many avalanches occurred after 1860 in America when men swarmed to the Sierra Nevada mountains to prospect for gold. The mining activities of the men—indeed the sound of their voices alone—were often enough to spark an avalanche. The impetus for investigation of avalanches has been heightened with the boom in skiing and other extreme sports in mountain ranges and, thankfully, there has been a huge increase in hazard education and the death tolls have been cut.

In America there has been worrying recognition of the fact that while novice skiers are at risk it is the veterans who are most likely to be caught up in an avalanche. Advice from the experts can sometimes compound the problem. If the forecast claims only a moderate chance of avalanche many will take that to mean they are entirely safe.

People skiing familiar routes often neglect to take note of changing conditions. They herd together in groups—far more likely to trigger avalanches—rather than spacing themselves out. In addition to this, people are proven crowd-followers and tend to follow in the assumption that the leader knows the ropes. This may not necessarily be so. When people are cold and uncomfortable they make a dash for warm shelter and are tempted to cut corners on safety in the process. Some believe themselves to be equal to an avalanche, that is, they feel able to confront the risk and survive. Commercial pressures, too, may lead people to make questionable judgements about the state of the mountainside before setting off. The skier who has driven for hours, spent money on a hotel, and must shortly leave for work again falls into this category. Careful evaluation of the risks are ignored for the sake of the thrill. If the sky is blue, the sun shining, and the snow crisp, thoughts of avalanche slip far to the back of the mind. Even pointed danger signs like hollow-sounding snow or extensive cracks can be overlooked.

Other known causes for avalanches include thunderclaps, sonic booms from aircraft, pistol shots, the movement of animals, and the collapse of collections of snow on precipices, known as cornices.

There are some pieces of information that are crucial to the survival of skiers—experienced snow observers can now pinpoint certain pre-conditions that are likely to precede an avalanche and a knowledge of the dangers can often save lives. For example, north facing slopes are more likely to avalanche in winter while it is south facing slopes, with their expanses of snow toward a strengthening sun, that are treacherous in the spring. Smooth slopes, which lack trees and rocks to anchor the snow, are more prone to avalanches, and snow falling at a rate of 2.5 centimeters (one inch) per hour is more likely to avalanche. Always check weather forecasts before going on an expedition.

The majority of natural avalanches occur during snow storms so a basic precaution is never to embark on a cross-slope expedition during a blizzard.

A brief thaw creates a dangerous situation. When the temperatures fall to freezing once more—known as a "melt-freeze"—the surface takes on the smoothness of an icerink and fresh snow, called "windslab," will fail to adhere to it, building up until its slips down in a mighty mass. Landslides are caused in a similar way—when water or snow turns underlying shale into slippery clay the mass of soil, trees, and rocks on top is undermined and comes cascading down. In warm weather landslides pose a similar threat on the same mountains as avalanches do in winter.

Above: The shockwave caused by the thundering descent of snow is often as catastrophic as the avalanche itself.

Strong winds can also also re-distribute freshly fallen snow, creating windslab. Avalanche experts point out that snow collects on the leeward or sheltered sides of slopes where the inexperienced might seek protection. These places are ripe for avalanches.

The result is the same when there is a vast quantity of powdery snow, seemingly innocuous but equally as dangerous. Powder avalanches are accompanied by powerful shock waves created by the momentum of the fall and these alone are capable of destroying houses and killing people in their path. One avalanche blast in Australia blew eight freight carriages off their rails before the mass of snow even arrived. In 1962, the force of the air preceding an avalanche knocked down 150-year-old trees. This type of avalanche is known in the Alps as *staublawinen*.

Wet snow, which comes about during a thaw, is also an avalanche threat. As it thunders down a mountainside it will gather more snow as well as trees and boulders on its way. Just such an avalanche gathered a devastating 2.5 million tons of snow on its descent in Italy in 1885. In the Alps these are called *gundlawinen*.

Slopes between 30 degrees and 45 degrees are the most susceptible to avalanches (on steep slopes snow does not have the opportunity to accumulate), and they can be triggered both above and below the area of windslab—snow can be very difficult to predict. In common with the prediction of other natural disasters, the business of forecasting avalanches is a long way from being an exact science. There are no guarantees. It is common knowledge that each snow crystal is unique, so falls of snow are hugely varied and create numerous different conditions on the ground. Snow can be either ice hard or marshmallow soft, and every point in between. There is frozen snow that will crush and grainy snow that overwhelms. The Inuit people of the frozen north have more than 100 words for snow, reflecting its many guises.

The study of snowfall and avalanches has made skiing on recognized runs much safer. Resorts monitor the weather forecasts and the lie of the snow regularly and experienced snow patrollers will detonate small bombs or use artillery to start avalanches, in a technique pioneered by the Swiss. The armory also includes an "Avalauncher," a compressed air cannon specifically designed for service in the mountains. This is put into action hours before even the most eager skier will hit the slope as part of the war waged on these natural disasters. (Bombing snow is nothing new. It was done extensively in the Alps during World War I to engulf enemy troops, killing as many as 40,000.)

Through controlled explosions windslab is shifted with minimum danger. Further preventative measures include fences, walls, or wedges that help prevent the formation of windslab by impersonating the dense forests that once covered mountainsides before the desire for timber sealed their fate. For established wooded areas provide the best protection from avalanches. Known avalanche paths have been identified and receive special attention, yet the experts will tell you, all this is "hazard reduction" not "avalanche control."

Rescue work is benefiting from developments in new technology. Now it is possible to equip snow sportspeople with beacons which will emit a traceable signal even from beneath the snow (of course, this only works if people choose to take advantage by wearing it). One of the latest advances is the "Ava-Lung," a broad, hollow chamber sewn into the jacket which will extract oxygen from the surrounding snow, which is between 40 and 90 per cent air. The skier breathes through a tube and can do so for upward of one hour.

Trained sniffer dogs, usually of the German Shepherd or St Bernard variety, can lead rescue teams to an overwhelmed skier and, armed with long poles known as sounding rods, which are pushed down into the snow, experienced teams have a chance of locating buried bodies. However, the cries of those trapped are muffled by the snow and time is short. Only a fraction of those caught up in avalanches are rescued alive. While there is a 90 per cent chance of survival for those pulled out within 15 minutes this diminshes to 30 per cent after 35 minutes.

If you are caught up in an avalanche, make swimming motions with your arms in order to reach the top of the snow flow. Hard as it may be, curb the desire to cry out or open your mouth to avoid inhalation of snow and as the descent ends keep your hands in front of your face to preserve an airspace. Companions of those buried in avalanches are instantly rescue workers. It falls to them to mark the spot where the victim was last seen and judge the fall line. Unless help is close by, stay at the scene. Those who decide further aid is imperative should mark the route they have followed so a rescue party can trace it back.

Death may occur immediately from wounds received as people are pulled down the mountainside at speed in the snow. The weight of snow bearing down on someone buried alive may crush them to death while inhalation of snow crystals can also kill. Those buried within an air pocket must be found before the oxygen runs out or before they freeze or starve to death—two hours is often as long as anyone can survive. Lamentably, some victims lay undiscovered until the spring thaw, their bodies remaining in lifeless perfection. After all, ice and snow are responsible for preserving the bodies of ancient people, giving archaeologists key clues to life thousands of years ago. Fortunately, the annual death toll is fairly small as the majority of avalanches are in remote regions.

The Alps is the most populated mountain region in the world and locals have responded to the threat of avalanches by building their homes with angular, reinforced walls to deflect snow flow.

FLOODS

Right: A serious flood such as this one will sweep away anything in its path. Even if some sturdy buildings survive, they will be so damaged that they are unsafe to live in. Flood damage can take months or even years to rectify.

At the end of winter the snows will thaw in an entirely natural process that has little impact on the surrounding countryside. But when there's been unusually heavy snow accompanied by torrential rain during the thaw then the chances of a flash flood occurring escalate. Floods can also be caused by fractured dams, earthquakes, volcanoes, landslides, hurricanes, extraordinarily large tides and tsunamis. The majority of all insurance claims following natural disasters are linked to flooding.

For years floods have claimed a huge human toll, and effects other than the initial inundation can be just as devastating. When waters rise they may erode the soil, kill livestock, damage sewers, undermine bridges, cause building subsidence, destroy wildlife habitats, deposit rocks and debris on agricultural fields, cause traffic delays, and wash out crops. Also, there's a risk of disease following a severe flood as well as the need for reconstruction, though it may take many weeks for a flood to subside far enough for rebuilding work to begin.

Low lying land is always at risk but the greatest floods will encompass higher ground as well. Past disasters have shown where people must defend themselves against flooding and engineers dictate in what form that happens. But water is immensely heavy and has unique strength—when it flows in a torrent, it can destroy everything in its path.

Since ancient times people have fought to keep the rivers and tides at bay with levees or raised embankments. Levees are used extensively on the Mississippi River in America in concert with other flood measures. All defence measures were useless, however, during the summer of 1993 when waters in the Mississippi and Missouri rivers burst their banks and flooded the surrounding countryside. The damage inflicted on the levees cost millions of dollars to put right. With 12 million acres of agricultural land under water as well as homes and businesses, the final bill was estimated at around 12 billion dollars.

Dams and artifically cut floodways help divert the water from areas at risk. Both Britain and the Netherlands have invested in massive storm surge barriers which are lowered when a sea flood is imminent.

The other side of floods is, of course, the creation of rich agricultural land after it has been fed by the river's sediment. For centuries, farmers around Egypt's River Nile exploited this resource and accepted river movements as a natural hazard. Since the construction of the Aswan High Dam which curbs the river's seasonal responses farmers have found their land much the poorer.

CYCLONES HURRICANES **TYPHOONS**

Above: About ten hurricanes are formed over the oceans each year and are the terror of coastal regions in their path.

There's danger too in the air. Cyclones, hurricanes, typhoons, and tornadoes are killers. The first three are essentially the same thing variously categorized by geographic location.

Cyclones are the fierce winds of the Indian Ocean and the south west Pacific. Hurricanes occur over the north Atlantic and eastern north Pacific while typhoons visit the western north Pacific.

The winds move in a circular manner, anti-clockwise, in the northern hemisphere and clockwise in the southern hemisphere. They originate in latitudes between five degrees and 20 degrees north and south of the equator (the doldrums) where water temperatures are in excess of 27 degrees centigrade. Warm air rises and sucks cooler air in at the bottom. Air pressure is low, a storm whips up and its spiraling action occurs because of the earth's rotation.

To earn the title of hurricane the tempest must be moving at speeds in excess of 120 kilometers per hour (74 miles per hour). This is the lowest grade of hurricane and is considered weak in meteorological terms. The highest have wind speeds of 250 kilometers per hour (155 miles per hour) or more and when hurricanes of this order strike they are devastating.

These storms have "eyes" where air pressure is at its lowest, a focus at the center measuring between 5 and 50 kilometers (three and 30 miles) in diameter that has calm and warm conditions. Yet the fiercest winds are those that circulate at the edge of the storm's eye, the highest being around 350 kilometers per hour (220 miles per hour). Water vapour condenses and manifests as heavy rain on the outer clouds.

Cyclone fronts (widths) can measure for scores or even hundreds of kilometers—Hurricane Felix, which arrived on America's Atlantic coast in August 1995, was some 500 kilometers (300 miles) wide.

The lifespan of a cyclone can range from several days to two weeks, during which time it will travel from its birthplace on an erratic path. Sometimes cyclones will remain in tropical water, but they may be swept along by weather troughs. About ten are formed each year, terrorizing shipping in particular. For instance, it is believed that the power of Typhoon Orchid was responsible for the sinking of the *Derbyshire* on September 10, 1980, in the China Sea. *Derbyshire* was a giant carrier, measuring 300 meters (1,000 feet) in length and 45 meters (145 feet) wide. She was laden with 157,000 tons of iron ore.

Yet *Derbyshire* went to the bottom so swiftly it seems there was not enough time even to issue a distress call and all 44 aboard were killed. An inquiry decided she was overwhelmed by the extreme weather conditions (though relatives of the victims believed the construction of the *Derbyshire* may have been at fault). There was nothing wrong with the way the *Wahine* was built, however, yet this sturdy ferry was tossed on to the rocks at the mouth of Wellington harbor in New Zealand after falling into the clutches of cyclone winds on April 11, 1968, and more than 50 passengers and crew died. When it hits land, a hurricane can cause havoc—telegraph poles are snapped like flower stems, buildings are torn from their foundations, yachts are flipped like pancakes. But coastal areas suffer the worst of the wrath—shorelines are battered by mighty waves, sea surges can raise the level of the sea by several meters, and, if the coast is low lying, then there is always extensive flooding. Bangladesh is perhaps the worst hit country in the world for three quarters of it lies at sea level and millions of people dwell in the river delta making a living on the fertile land there. Typhoons and the accompanying surge have cost the lives of millions.

TORNADOES

Tornadoes are, like cyclones, caused by the collision of warm and cool air, this time over land, spawning storm cells. The result is a rapidly-spinning trunk or funnel which descends from angry clouds down to earth—nick-named a twister. Meteorologists still don't know precisely why tornadoes act as they do, although low pressure, high winds, updraughts, and weather fronts all play a part in their formation.

America is no stranger to the spectacle of an all-consuming tornado. Nationwide, the country experiences about 1,000 each year although January 1999 was a record breaker with 169 tornadoes touching down in that month alone, claiming 18 lives. On one day alone—January 21—87 twisters were reported, 38 of them in Arkansas.

There's a stretch of land encompassing Texas, Arkansas, Oklahoma, Kansas, Nebraska, and the Dakotas which has earned the title "Tornado Alley" due to the frequency of the phenomena. Above those states, warm moist air from the Gulf of Mexico combines with cold air from Canada and thus tornadoes are created.

The state most visited by tornadoes is Texas where fortunately the wide open spaces ensure that at least a proportion harmlessly blow themselves out. That's why the state suffering the most deaths from tornadoes per 10,000 square meters is the more densely populated Massachusetts.

Three quarters of all tornadoes are weak in velocity. The wind speeds are as low as 65 kilometers per hour (40 miles per hour) and it is trees, chimneys, and sign posts that bear the brunt of these. The Fujita Scale, which is an accepted measure of tornadoes, terms these as gale tornadoes. After gale comes moderate, which blow at 117-180 kilometers per hour (73-112 miles per hour), then significant, 181-252 kilometers per hour (113-157 miles per hour), severe, 253-331 kilometers per hour (158-206 miles per hour), devastating, 332-418 kilometers per hour (207-260 miles per hour), incredible, 419-511 kilometers per hour (261-318 miles per hour), and finally inconceivable, 512-609 kilometers per hour (319-379 miles per hour), although the latter are very rare.

Violent tornadoes are few in number but catastrophic in effect. They are capable of flattening homes, overturning cars, and transforming household equipment like refridgerators into missiles. The scale of damage can be misleading—the tell-tale sign of a tornado's strength is the size of debris it throws about.

It is also worth remembering that the size of a tornado does not indicate its strength; a large tornado may be weak while a small one can be exceedingly strong. Tornado energy is soon expended and they can be over in a matter of minutes or even seconds, with the longest lasting twister on record enduring for just three and a half hours. This means they usually only travel a mile or two before disappearing although rare

cases report a distance in excess of 160 kilometers (100 miles). The path left by a tornado is typically 45 meters (150 feet) wide but, once again, every twister is different and it can be greater.

How can you tell when a tornado is brewing? The sky is heavy with green, gray, and black clouds that scud at an unnaturally fast pace or circle one another. The air is filled with a roar or even a scream, similar to that issued by a low flying jet plane—the word tornado is from the Latin *tonare* meaning to thunder—and often lightning is apparent in the clouds and even the funnel. Few could fail to notice the impressive and terrifying funnel which comprises dust and condensation but be warned, it isn't always visible. Sometimes the only clue to its whereabouts is the debris spinning skywards. Generally, although not always, twisters travel from the south west to the north east.

For those who live in areas susceptible to tornadoes it is as well to identify a safe place in which to hide. A basement is ideal or an inner bathroom where the bath itself might provide essential protection from flying furniture. There are also storm shelters designed specifically for the purpose. Choosing refuge beneath stairs or under a strong table is also a sensible option. Taking to the car in an attempt to outrun the tornado is ill-advised as it is notoriously difficult to know just where it is heading and residents of mobile homes should quit before the the winds hit. In the face of 160 kilometer per hour (100 mile per hour) winds, mobile homes will disintegrate.

A rumor has persisted in America for years that it is advisable to open all windows, apparently to reduce pressure in a building. It is actually possible that air will rush in and blow out the building like a balloon. Home owners should close windows and stay well away from them as they could shatter. Another widely held belief is that the south west corner of a basement remains the safest for shelter during a tornado. That perceived wisdom surely emanates from the 1887 publication *Tornadoes* by John Park Finley which states: "Under no circumstances, whether in a building or in a cellar, ever take a position in a northeast room, in a northeast corner or in an east room or against an east wall." Research carried out 80 years afterward has proved that this is nonsense.

Whirlwinds are close cousins of tornadoes but generally far smaller and less alarming. Meteorologically speaking, they are the atmospheric phenomena familiarly called dust devils or dust whirls which occur over deserts and plains on hot, calm days. Nevertheless, their height may still be in excess of 90 meters (300 feet) though 1,500 meter (5,000 feet) dust whirlwinds have been seen, but are rare. They can last from just a few seconds to several hours.

TAUPO NEW ZEALAND
c. AD130 VOLCANO

Much of what occurred when Taupo erupted nearly 2,000 years ago is conjecture. But informed guesses claim that no less than 30 million tons of pumice was pumped out of the volcano, at speeds of up to 650 kilometers per hour (400 miles per hour). The major clue comes in the spread of the debris which indicates the power of the driving force behind it. Most of the pumice fell more than 200 kilometers (125 miles) from the volcano.

VESUVIUS ITALY
August 24, AD79 VOLCANO

Right: Residents of Pompeii flee for their lives in a 19th century depiction of the city's ruin during an eruption of Mount Vesuvius, in AD79.

When Vesuvius erupted, while Imperial Rome was at the zenith of its power, it coated the town of Herculaneum with thick mud and submerged Pompeii, some distance to the south, with a sheet of volcanic ash. Numerous smaller settlements were obliterated at the same time. The death toll is estimated at about 2,000.

For centuries the sites remained virtually undisturbed, but for a few treasure hunters of the 17th century. It is here that the preservative powers of volcanic lava and ash are so amply illustrated as items captured in the flow failed to deteriorate during the passing centuries. Everything from entire buildings to inconsequential everyday items like pots and wooden window shutters were revealed by archaeological digs. While the volcano's activity that night was an unmitigated disaster for the local population around the Bay of Naples it became a priceless gift to later generations who were finally able to make satisfactory conclusions about life in the Roman empire.

Although the remains of Herculaneum were discovered as long ago as 1709, excavation of the site is still far from complete. The amphitheater has been disinterred, as have numerous streets and houses. The treasures yielded also include a child's cot, detailed mosaics, and a library of 1,800 books.

Archaeological exploration of Pompeii began in the 1740s. Here the theater, public baths, basilica, arches, paved walkways, homes, even gardens, were brought to light. Graffiti and advertisements were also found.

The eruption claimed the life of Pliny the Elder (23-79AD) who was so fascinated by volcanoes that he insisted on visiting Stabaie at the heart

CITY OF NAPLES, AND ERUPTION OF VESUVIUS.

Above: This 19th century engraving shows the smoking peak of Vesuvius, which has been active for thousands of years.

Right: Ruins of the Roman city of Pompeii, destroyed by Mount Vesuvius in 79AD. The volcano stands on the horizon.

of the danger zone to witness the scene first hand. He was ultimately suffocated by poison gases.

In a letter about the incident his nephew Pliny the Younger (62-113), who watched the eruption from Capo Miseno, 30 kilometers (20 miles) distant reported:

"There had been for several days some shocks from earthquakes, which hardly alarmed us because they are frequent in Campania; but that night they became so violent that one might think that the world was not being merely shaken, but turned upside-down . . . Outside the houses we found ourselves in the midst of a strange and terrible scene. The coaches we had ordered out, though upon level ground, were sliding to and fro, and could not be kept steady . . . Then we saw the sea sucked back and, as it were, repulsed by the convulsive motion of the earth . . . and now many sea animals were captive on dry land . . . On the other side, a black and dreadful cloud bursting out in gusts of igneous serpentine vapor now and again yawned open to reveal long, fantastic flames, resembling flashes of lightning but much larger. Soon afterwards the cloud I have described began to descend upon the earth and to cover the sea . . . My mother beseeched me to escape as best I might: a young man could do it; she, burdened by age and corpulency, would die easy if only she had not caused my death. I replied I would not be saved without her . . . I looked behind me. A gross darkness pressed upon our rear and came rolling over the land as a torrent . . . We had scarce sat down when darkness over-spread us, not like that of a moonless or cloudy night, but of a room when it is shut up, and the lamp put out. You could hear the shrieks of women, the crying of children, the shouts of men . . . I might have boasted that amidst dangers so appalling, not a sigh or expression of fear escaped me, had not my support been founded on that miserable consolation that all mankind were involved in the same calamity."

SHAANXI CHINA
February 2, 1556 **EARTHQUAKE**

Shaanxi has the unenviable accolade of recording the most fatalities in an earthquake in the history of the world. There were an estimated 830,000 deaths when the earth shook violently in the region, a number that has never been surpassed since. The total is of course open to question as records on both fatalities and population were less fastidiously kept than they are today. However, it is known that a cliff of soft windblown silt called "loess" was providing homes to countless peasants who had carved themselves caves within it for shelter. Loess can usually be relied upon to remain firm but under duress from the earthquake it collapses in dense heaps.

TEIDE TENERIFE
May 5, 1706 **VOLCANO**

Bory de Saint-Vincent describes the destruction of the town of Guarrachico during the 1706 eruption of Teide, Tenerife:

"Guarrachico was a pleasant town, surrounded with fertile fields and rich vineyards . . . During the night of May 5, 1706, a noise was heard underground like that of a storm, and the sea retreated. When the day broke, and rendered visible the phenomenon, the peak was seen covered with a fearful red vapor. The air was on fire, a sulphurous smell suffocated the frightened animals. The waters were covered with steam similar to that over the boiling springs; all at once the earth moved and opened; torrents of lava flowed from the crater of Teide, and rushed into the plains from the north west. The town, half swallowed up in the clefts in the ground, half buried by the vomited lava, disappeared entirely. The sea, returning to its bed, inundated the ruins of the port, which had sunk down; waves and heaps of cinders occupy the site of Guarrachico. The inhabitants tried to save themselves by immediate flight, but most of them made futile attempts; some were swallowed up in the clefts, buried alive; others, suffocated by the sulphurous vapors, fell asphyxiated in their attempts to escape. Many of these unfortunates, however, escaped with much peril, and seeing from far their homes in flames, flattered themselves with the hope that they had escaped, when nearly all were crushed by a hail of enormous stones, the last effect of the eruption."

LANZAROTE CANARY ISLANDS
September 1, 1730 **VOLCANO**

Beaches in the holiday resorts of the Canary Islands, off the coast of Africa, are black with volcanic ash. The islands have a long history of volcanic activity and, for six years between 1730 and 1736, were shaken by the emergence of a series of volcanoes. An eyewitness account exists by the hand of one Don Andres Lorenzo Curbelo which records the terror faced by the local farmers:

"On that first night an enormous mountain arose from the bosom of the earth and from its summit there escaped flames that continued to burn for nineteen days . . . The lava spread over villages to the north, at first as rapidly as water but soon its speed slowed so that it glowed more like honey.

"On January 7, 1731, further eruptions devastated the earlier ones. Incandescent currents, accompanied by very thick smoke, came out of two openings formed in the mountain. The clouds of smoke were frequently lit by brilliant flashes of a blue and red light, followed by violent thunderclaps, like in storms, and this spectacle was as terrifying as it was new for the inhabitants because storms are unknown in these lands.

"The earth continued to vomit its incandescent basalt until April 16, 1736, engulfing a surface of 20 square miles, covering fields and villages, destroying 400 houses, and building more than 30 cones that were all aligned on a gigantic fissure. The western quarter of the island, once so fertile and flourishing, was annihilated."

LISBON PORTUGAL
November 1, 1755 **EARTHQUAKE**

When Lisbon was struck by a series of earthquakes, one third of Europe shuddered—an area of about two million square kilometers (1,300,000 square miles). Neighboring Spain was most severely hit with buildings toppling under the strain, but the tremors were felt as far away as Scotland and Sweden.

None of this could detract from the horrors that faced the Portuguese capital where a third of the population died—the death toll was in the order of 50,000. Those who survived the horror of the earthquake were then challenged by the might of a tsunami measuring between six and 15 meters (20 and 50 feet) in height. It was one of the few tsunamis to rear up in the Atlantic Ocean. Its momentum carried it as far north as Holland and as far west as to be a four meter (12 feet) swell in the West Indies.

This appalling disaster proved a tremendous challenge to the faith of many who felt bound to question why God had inflicted such terrible punishment on a region renowned for the devout nature of its citizens— the Catholic Church found it difficult to claim "hand of God."

Fortunately for the faith, the Lisbon earthquake marked the beginning of official studies of the phenomena, which in turn led to the view that earthquakes were natural rather than supernatural occurrences. Eyewitness accounts were collected from priests in the area and were studied by John Michell, an English physicist who concluded that waves had been sent through the ground. There was, he assured, no evidence of divine intervention.

VESUVIUS ITALY
June 19, 1794 **VOLCANO**

Right: Lava courses down the snow-covered slopes of Vesuvius during the eruption of 1794.

Vesuvius flexed its muscle twice in 30 years during the latter half of the 18th century. During the first eruption, in 1764, a series of rumblings and pumice showers culminated in a four-hour long explosion which split the night in Naples. As the ash rain grew more dense and the explosions continued unabated, the anxious population prevailed upon the local cardinal to bring the most important religious relic of the region—the head of St Januarius—from its resting place to lead a procession towards the violent volcano. Bystanders insist the volcano became calm again as soon as the saint came within sight.

In 1794, the volcano once more exercised its might, this time causing the destruction of the town of Torre del Greco, which lay south east of the mountain, north of Pompeii. Sir William Hamilton, husband of Lady Emma Hamilton (the mistress of Admiral Lord Nelson) and a prominent vulcanologist reported it thus:

". . . the residue of the lava . . . flowed upon Torre presenting a front from 1,200 feet to 1,500 feet in breadth and filling several deep ravines.

"On reaching the first houses of the town the stream divided according to the different slopes of the streets and the degrees of opposition presented by the buildings.

"... The vast clouds of thick, black smoke which rose from the town, the flames occasionally crowning the summit of the houses, the ruins of the buildings, the noise of the falling palaces and houses, the rumbling of the volcano—these were the principal incidents of the horrible yet sublime scene."

LAKI ICELAND
Summer, 1783 **VOLCANO**

It was a bleak summer in Iceland after Mount Skaptar spewed sufficient lava to fill an 80 kilometer (50 mile) river valley to depths of between 30 and 180 meters (100 and 600 feet). In all, 20 villages were submerged by the molten tide which soon covered an area totaling 520 square kilometers (200 square miles). Worse, the sulfurous cloud from the volcano spread further still, killing off crops and suffocating livestock. It became impossible to make a living from the land on a sizeable section of that rural island and the death toll from ash fall, poisonous gases, and the ensuing famine was 10,500, about one fifth of the population.

TAMBORA INDONESIA
April 5, 1815 **VOLCANO**

Facts about the volcano eruption at Tambora are hazy but it is generally accepted that the consequent loss of life was colossal. It seems that this hitherto unremarkable volcano on the island of Sumbawa, west of Java, exploded with several detonations that could be heard hundreds of miles away. The eruption was so powerful that blocks of rock were hurled 40 kilometers (25 miles). Its accompanying ash smog was so dense that it blotted out the sun for three days and the choking cloud which rained down hot rocks on the inhabitants beneath killed about 12,000. The famine which followed the destruction of the fields claimed the lives of a further 80,000.

Sir Stamford Raffles, better known for his involvement in Far Eastern politics, reported on the eruption of Tambora in 1815:

"The eruption began on April 5th and did not quite cease until July. There were first detonations, which were heard in Sumatra, a distance of nearly 931 miles, and were taken for discharges of artillery. Three distinct columns of flame rose to an immense height, and the whole surface of the mountain soon appeared covered with incandescent lava, which extended to enormous distances; stones, some as large as the head, fell in a circle of several miles diameter, and the fragments dispersed in the air caused total darkness . . . The explosion lasted 34 days, and the abundance of the ashes expelled was such that at Java, a distance of 310 miles, they caused complete darkness in midday, and covered the ground and roofs with stratum several inches thick. At Sambawa also, the region near the volcano was entirely devastated, and the houses destroyed with 12,000 inhabitants. Thirty-six persons only escaped the disaster. The trees and pasturages were buried deeply under pumice and ashes. At Bima, 40 miles from the volcano, the weight of the ashes was such that the roofs were crushed in. The floating pumice in the sea formed an island three feet in thickness, that the vessels could scarcely pass through."

COSEGUINA NICARAGUA
January, 1835 VOLCANO

An eyewitness account of the eruption of Coseguina, Nicaragua, from the commandant of La Union, El Salvador, 50 kilometers (31 miles) north of the volcano:

"On the 20th, the day dawned with its usual serenity until 8 o'clock, when a rumbling noise preceded a dense cloud that rose like a pyramid towards the southeast, until it covered the sun. By 11, the whole sky was covered, and we were enveloped in the greatest darkness, unable to see even the nearest objects . . . Everything combined to fill the stoutest souls with fear, even more so at 4 o'clock, when the earth began to quake and to continue a perpetual shaking which gradually increased. This was followed by a shower of phosphoric sand until 8 o'clock, when there began a heavy fall of powder-like flour. Thunder and lightning continued the whole night and the following day . . . The darkness lasted 43 hours, and it was indispensable for us to carry a light, even if it was not sufficient to see with . . . From dawn on the 23rd, a dim sunlight showed the uneven streets quite level, being covered with dust. Men, women and children were so disfigured that it was not easy to recognize anyone except by their voices or other circumstances . . . At 10 o'clock we were again plunged into darkness . . . and, though leaving brought immediate peril from wild beasts fleeing the forests, . . . more than half the inhabitants of La Union emigrated on foot, abandoning their houses, well persuaded that they should never return to them."

ELM SWITZERLAND
September 11, 1883 **LANDSLIDE**

Careless quarrying appears to have been the cause of the landslip in Switzerland which killed 115. After heavy rains, the east side of the mountain sheared away and tumbled into the valley below. Moving at an estimated speed of 145 kilometers per hour (90 miles per hour), the tons of rubble hit the valley floor and climbed 275 meters (900 feet) up the other side before coming to a halt. It covered the ground to a depth of some 14 meters (45 feet).

KRAKATOA JAVA
August 27, 1883 **VOLCANO**

Right: A contemporary engraving of Krakatoa before the incredibly violent eruption devastated the island.

The explosion at Krakatoa was, quite simply, the mightiest ever—26 times more powerful than the largest H-bomb ever tested on the planet. Krakatoa, also known by the Indonesian name of Krakatau or Rakata, was a small, uninhabited island lying in the waterway that separated Java and Sumatra. (Mystifyingly, American film-makers who, in 1968, made an adventure movie set against the backdrop of the eruption called it *Krakatoa, East of Java* when in fact it lies to the west.) That the volcano was going to "blow its top" was fully expected. It had done so once before, in 1680, and this time, tell-tale rumbles had been heard since May 20. But no one was prepared for such violent ferocity when at last the pressure became too great for the 46 square kilometer (18 square mile) island to contain any longer. There were a series of explosions, one producing one of the loudest noises in history, heard some 5,000 kilometers (3,000 miles) away and debris shot 55 kilometers (34 miles) into the air. The cloud of volcanic dust was so dense that it was still visible in the upper atmosphere three years later, intensifying the colors of sunrises and sunsets. It is said the shock wave created by the volcano traveled around the globe seven times before it faded. The volcano top collapsed into a basin formation. However, the most significant effect of the Krakatoa eruption in human terms was the tsunami that followed. Pyroclastic flow plunging into the sea coupled with a submarine earthquake displaced the water that formed the tsunami. Typically, it raced along the deep sea without causing too much trouble until arriving at the coastal shallows. Now its height built to some 27 meters (120 feet) and it swallowed up some 163 villages and their 36,000 residents in Java and Sumatra. Waves caused by the earthquakes traveled some 13,000

kilometers (8,000 miles) around the globe to give sizeable swell in the far distant English Channel. In 1927, volcanic eruptions occured once more in the area. A new island called Anak Krakatau—child of Krakatau—rose from the waves the following year and had reached a height of 190 meters (622 feet) above sea level in 1973.

YELLOW RIVER CHINA
September 1887 FLOOD

The world's most devastating flood occurred when the waters of the Hwang Ho, or Yellow River, topped levees that were 20 meters (70 feet) high. It had long been a treacherous neighbor to the peasants living by its banks; floods from this 5,000 kilometer (3,000 mile) long river which rises in Tibet and heads for the Yellow Sea were a regular occurrence. Yet farmers continued to live in its shadow for, with each flood, the ground grew more fertile. This time, however, the flood exceeded all expectations. Water spilled over some 130,000 square kilometers (50,000 square miles), wiping out 300 villages and killing between one and six million. A further two million were left homeless.

JOHNSTOWN USA
May 31, 1889 FLOOD

When the walls of a neglected dam split open, a mighty wall of water came down on an industrial town and surrounding villages claiming at least 2,000 lives. Telegraph poles snapped like twigs in the torrent, locomotives bumped along like flotsam. Nothing could resist such a colossal force. One eyewitness account told how the dam "just melted away."

"Only a few minutes were required to make an opening more than 300 feet wide and down to the bottom. I watched it until the wall that held back the waters was torn away, and the entire lake began to move, and finally, with a tremendous rush that made the hills quake, the vast body of water was poured out into the valley below. Only about 45 minutes were required to precipitate those millions of tons of water upon the unsuspecting inhabitants of the Conemaugh valley."

Afterwards, construction and maintenance standards for dams across the USA were radically overhauled.

ASSAM INDIA
June 12, 1897 EARTHQUAKE

Such was the force of the Great Assam earthquake that buildings in Calcutta some 320 kilometers (200 miles) from its focus were destroyed and people living 1,450 kilometers (900 miles) away were aware of earth movements. The ground was fractured leaving a ten meter (35 feet) high cliff. Its magnitude, according to the Richter Scale, was a phenomenal 8.7 and thousands of lives were lost. The same area was subject to another mighty quake on August 15, 1950. It caused landslides, flooding, and a tsunami which made its presence felt as far away as northern Europe. An estimated 1,500 people were killed by tremors, the greatest of which measured 8.6 on the Richter Scale.

MOUNT PELÉE MARTINIQUE
May 8, 1902 VOLCANO

Few have cause for celebration when they are behind bars. M. Cyparis was one of that lucky breed for, while in jail on a charge of drunkeness, he escaped from the cataclysmic eruption of Mt Pelée, which killed some 28,000 of his fellow inhabitants in the sea port of St Pierre, Martinique. The cell he inhabited, although rank, windowless, and deep underground, proved to be his savior. No poisonous fumes reached him there, while his friends and neighbors were killed by asphyxiation. Warning signs from the trembling mountain—the muffled thundering and earth tremors—were largely ignored by the people of St Pierre. They knew that the volcano of La Soufrière on the nearby island of St Vincent had erupted. Although 1,500 people had died it was generally held to be a good omen, that the pressure would be defused in the volcano that stood five miles from their own town. It wasn't to be. One May morning there was a blinding flash. Before they had a chance to escape the townsfolk were engulfed in a poisonous cloud. The eruption laid waste to the town, reducing buildings to smoking rubble, and 17 ships anchored offshore were sunk. A sailor on the British steamship *Roraima*, one of the few out-lying vessels which escaped destruction, recorded the volcano as follows:

"The flames were . . . spurting up in the air, now and then waving to one side or the other for a moment and again leaping suddenly higher up.

"There was a constant muffled roar. It was like the biggest oil refinery in the world burning up on the mountain top. . . . The mountain was blown to pieces. There was no warning. The side of the volcano was ripped out and there was hurled straight towards us a solid wall of flame. It sounded like thousands of cannon."

Shoemaker Leon Compère-Léandre was one of only four known survivors of the disaster:

"On May 8th, at about eight o'clock in the morning, I was seated on the doorstep of my house, which was in the southeast part of the town. All of a sudden I felt a terrible wind blowing, the Earth began to tremble, and the sky suddenly became dark. I turned to go into the house, made with great difficulty the three or four steps that separated me from my room, and felt my arms and legs burning, also my body. I dropped upon a table. At this moment, four others sought refuge in my room, crying and writhing with pain, although their garments showed no sign of having been touched by flame. At the end of 10 minutes one of these, the young Delavaud girl, aged 10 fell dead; the others left. I then got up and went

Above Right: Villagers stare as Mt Pelée erupts. Tragically there were only a handful of survivors after poisonous gases engulfed the region.

Below Right: A few people cower before a huge cloud of black smoke and ash during the eruption of Mt Pelée. The eruption destroyed a city and killed thousands in Martinique, 1902.

Far Right: A man sitting on Orange Hill surveys the ruins of the town of Saint Pierre after the eruption of Mt Pelée.

into another room, where I found the father, Delavaud, still clothed and lying on the bed, dead. He was purple and inflated, but the clothing was intact. I went out and found in the court two corpses interlocked; they were the bodies of the two young men who had been with me in the room. Re-entering the house, I came upon the bodies of two men who had been in the garden when I returned to my house at the beginning of the catastrophe. Crazed and almost overcome, I threw myself upon a bed, inert and awaiting death."

GALVESTON TEXAS
September 8, 1900 **HURRICANE**

Above: Damage caused by the hurricane and strom surge in Galveston. This was the greatest natural disaster in terms of loss of life in US history.

The perils of inhabiting low lying coastland were never more apparent than when Hurricane Alicia hit the Texas town of Galveston. Although its foundations were, quite literally, built in the sand on an island off the shore, the town was prosperous both as a port and a center for the cotton trade. Golden weather gave way to storm conditions on the morning of September 8. After pounding waves ate their way through the beaches and covered the sole bridge linking the island to the mainland the people of Galveston knew a crisis loomed. With the ground under water they took to the buildings, many of them brick built and apparently stout, including the Sacred Heart Church. Alas, the foundations failed to hold fast. Few of the town's buildings could withstand the winds of the hurricane which thundered through at 180 kilometers per hour (110 mile per hour). They endured hours of appalling battering, broken only by a short spell in the middle when the eye of the storm passed over them bringing tranquility and clear skies. Those who were sufficiently misled to leave their shelters soon discovered, to their cost, this was a temporary lull. The death toll was 6,000, about a sixth of the population. On the mainland a similar number were killed. Galveston, including its Sacred Heart Church, was destroyed. When the city was rebuilt, lessons had been learned and a sea wall was included to fend off rising seas so that Texas need never again suffer so devastatingly from the forces of a hurricane.

TAHITI
February 8, 1906 **TYPHOON**

About 10,000 people were believed killed when a cyclone with 190 kilometer per hour (120 mile per hour) winds whipping up 20 meter (65 feet) high waves struck Tahiti. Whole islands were submerged in the melée and scores of villages were wiped out. The neighboring Society and Cook islands in the vicinity endured a similar lashing.

SAN FRANCISCO CALIFORNIA USA
April 18, 1906 **EARTHQUAKE**

Dawn brought with it a rude awakening. Shortly after 5 am there was a foreshock—the warning that worse was to come. Half a minute later an earthquake calculated at 7.8 on the Richter Scale let rip. The violent shaking of the quake which lasted for about a minute and the conflagration that ensued, reduced the city of San Francisco to smoking rubble. Earthquake trauma subsequently became etched into the national consciousness, in much the same way as the Boston Tea Party and the assassination of President John F. Kennedy, and this quake is the benchmark by which other American disasters are measured.

The earth ruptured along a 480 kilometer (300 mile) stretch that morning and its effects were felt from Oregon to Nevada. But its epicenter was San Francisco and it is here that most of the damage was

Below Left: This overview of the streets and buildings of San Francisco, taken on the 57th anniversary of the San Francisco earthquake of 1906, gives an idea of how built up the city was at the time of the disaster.

Bottom Left: This photograph contrasts dramatically with the one above—much of San Francisco was reduced to rubble by the huge tremors.

Handwritten text on image:
Photo and Copyright by
Geo R Lawrence Co, Chicago
1906
"San Francisco In Ruins"
May 5th 1906

Above: San Francisco after it had been leveled by the earthquake and accompanying fire of 1906.

wrought. A death toll of 700 is now believed to be underestimated—recent research puts the figure at around 3,000. Earthquake and fire combined to destroy about 28,000 buildings, rendering 225,000 people homeless. (Further damage was caused when firefighters used dynamite to blow up surviving buildings in a vain attempt to stem the flames.) In cash terms, the disaster cost in the region of 400 million (4 billion) dollars. One journalist eyewitness told how, during the foreshock, "the pavement pulsated like a living thing. Around me the huge buildings, looming up more terrible because of the queer dance they were performing wobbled and veered. Crash followed crash and resounded on all sides." When the main earthquake struck, the reporter was petrified:

"It made me think of the loved ones in different portions of the country. It turned my stomach, gave me a heartache that I will never forget and caused me to sink upon my knees and pray to the Almighty God that me and mine should escape the awful fate I knew was coming to so many thousands."

It is a popular misconception that martial law was declared by an anxious President Roosevelt although no telegram saying as much exists in the archives. Nevertheless, troops took to the streets to maintain order among the dispossessed. A newspaper report submits:

"During the afternoon three thieves met their death by rifle bullets while at work in the ruins. The curious were driven back at the breasts of the horses that the cavalrymen rode and all the crowds were forced from the level district to the hilly section beyond to the north."

Writer Jack London, author of *The Call of the Wild*, was horrified by what he saw when he arrived from his home 65 kilometers (40 miles) away:

"San Francisco is gone. Nothing remains of it but memories and a fringe of dwelling-houses on its outskirts.

"Within an hour after the earthquake shock the smoke of San Francisco's burning was a lurid tower visible a hundred miles away. And for three days and nights this lurid tower swayed in the sky, reddening the sun, darkening the day and filling the land with smoke."

Above: The aftermath of the 1906 San Francisco earthquake. Few buildings are left standing in what was previously a busy metropolis.

Left: Shelters for the homeless, which were erected in the ruins of San Francisco.

Far Left: Emergency food piled in San Francisco's Jefferson Square Park.

VALPARAISO CHILE
August 18, 1906 **EARTHQUAKE**

Its name translates to "Paradise Valley." Yet never was a place so ineptly named as that picturesque port after an earthquake leveled two thirds of its buildings. The earthquake—even more powerful than the one in San Francisco just a few months before—occurred at night. Terrified people who fled their homes were quickly drenched by a violent rainstorm which accompanied the disaster.

KINGSTON JAMAICA
January 22, 1907 **EARTHQUAKE**

Above Right: The ruins of the Royal Mail Steamship's building after the earthquake in Kingston, Jamaica, 1907.

Below Right: Workers in Kingston carry away debris from the damaged buildings.

It's an earthquake remembered not so much for the hundreds killed or the devastation wrought over a 16 kilometer (10 mile) radius but for the high-handed attitude of a colonialist bureaucrat. Jamaica's British Governor, Sir J. A. Sweetenham, turned down an immediate offer of medicine and food from a visiting American fleet. He chose instead to wait for two British ships to arrive with supplies despite the huge numbers of hungry and injured around him. There was an outcry both in America and Britain at his actions. Within six weeks Sweetenham had resigned over mismanagement of the disaster.

1907

MESSINA SICILY
December 28, 1907 **EARTHQUAKE**

Below Right: Townspeople carry an injured person away on a stretcher, after an earthquake devastated Messina, Sicily, in 1907.

Bottom Right: Survivors of the Messina earthquake lift a corpse on a stretcher.

Far Right: The ruins of a street in Messina. In all, some 75,000 people perished in the disaster.

The earth had been grinding and growling for two years in spectacular fashion. Yet if people believed it had expended its energy during three major earthquakes in as many years they were too easily fooled. The planet had held something in reserve and Messina at the foot of Italy was the unlucky recipient of its ire.

When the earth trembled, bringing the Christmas season to a swift end, about 75,000 perished. It was the largest earthquake ever known in Europe. Survivors then endured the wrath of a tsunami, which further added to the devastation. The plight of the homeless during those winter months was pitiful, the relief brought in by the Italian government all too slow in taking effect.

Left: The Sicily earthquake caused
devastation around the whole island,
these mountainside ruins were once
the thriving village of Gibellina.

WELLINGTON WASHINGTON USA
March 1, 1910 **AVALANCHE**

America's worst avalanche disaster occurred in the Cascade Mountains when a railway station and three trains were swept away. Snow had already been on the move that day, blocking the line leading over Stevens Pass and passengers were doubtless feeling the chill as their trains stood idle. Suddenly an avalanche launched itself, powering through the station. It took the building, together with the three waiting locomotives, and a number of carriages over a ledge and down 45 meters (150 feet) into a canyon below. By the time the whistling tide of snow had come to a halt 118 people had died. The railway company was faced with substantial damage. Afterwards millions of dollars was spent re-routing the track through a tunnel so that the vagaries of the winter weather could no longer take such a terrible toll.

NOVARUPTA
June, 1912 **Volcano**

In June 1912, Captain Perry of the US Coastguard cutter *Manning* observed the eruption of Novarupta from a distance of over 150 kilometrs (90 miles). Despite the distance, the experience was awful:

"All streams and wells have now become chocked, about five inches of ash having fallen, and water was furnished to the inhabitants by the *Manning* and by a schooner. At noon, ashes began to fall again, increased until 1.00 pm; visibility was about 50 feet. Abject terror took possession of the place. At 2.00 pm pitch darkness shut in. There were heavy static disturbances to the radio. No light appeared at dawn on June 8th. Ash had been removed from the ship on June 7th, but now decks, masts, yards, and lifeboats were loaded with flakes of fine dust of a yellowish color. Sulphurous fumes came at times in the air. Avalanches of ashes could be heard sliding on the neighboring hills sending forth clouds of suffocating dust. The crew kept at work with shovels, and four streams of water were kept playing incessantly to try to rid the ship of ash. The dust fell so heavily that a lantern could not be seen at arm's length."

KANSU PROVINCE CHINA
December 16, 1920 EARTHQUAKE

A bleak region near the Tibetan border was subject to wholesale destruction when an earthquake struck. Its effect was felt over an area of some 39,000 square kilometers (15,000 square miles), while the tremors registered in an area that measured a hundred times greater. Once again it was those living in areas of loess that fell victim to the disaster. The death toll was reported to be about 180,000. For the survivors the nightmare was re-lived just a dozen years later when another violent earthquake struck on December 26, 1932.

KANTO PLAIN JAPAN
September 1, 1923 EARTHQUAKE

The cities of Tokyo and Yokohama were both devastated when the Kanto province was shaken by an earthquake shortly before noon. The earthquake and the fires that followed killed 143,000, injured a further 100,000, and an estimated 500,000 buildings were destroyed. Fires raged for days as fire fighting equipment was destroyed and the water mains were shattered. The focus of the earthquake was under Sagami Bay, almost 100 kilometers (60 miles) southwest of Tokyo. Such was its velocity that the entire area moved in a southeasterly direction for distances of

Left: Locals begin the seemingly endless task of cleaning the streets after the Kanto Plain Earthquake.

up to four and a half meters (15 feet) and vertical shifts of up to two
meters (six feet). According to a Tokyo businessman who was in his office
at the time: "The shock was like a bucking horse, three great shakes. It
shot me out of my chair. I just missed being crushed by the safe." He went
on to describe how office buildings disappeared before his astonished
eyes and roofs and other debris covered the site where moments before
had stood a city. One unsavory aspect to the earthquake was the fate of
Koreans living in the Tokyo. Rumors abounded among the Japanese that
the Koreans were responsible for looting the shops and for arson. Their
response was to dispatch lynch mobs who claimed the lives of thousands.
In 1997, Tokyo marked the anniversary with "Earthquake Preparedness
Day" in which seven million residents took part in an earthquakedrill.

Above: In the wake of the Japanese earthquake, people flee the city taking with them what possessions they have managed to salvage.

Left: Victims walk through the devastated streets of Tokyo.

Overleaf: A scene of destruction showing the Nihonbashi ruins, Tokyo, after the 1923 earthquake.

MISSOURI/ ILLINOIS/ INDIANA USA
March 18, 1925 **TORNADO**

The "Tri-State Tornado" proved to be a defining moment in twister history. Never before had a tornado traveled so far, so fast, and claimed the lives of so many. It has never been beaten as America's worst ever single tornado. It journeyed some 350 kilometers (219 miles), was over a kilometer in width for the duration, and maintained a surprisingly straight course. This roaring killer distinguished itself by appearing sometimes as a double funnel twister and sometimes without a funnel apparent at all. Its average speed was 100 kilometers per hour (62 miles per hour). At its end 695 people lay dead and 2,000 were injured.

The death and destruction began in Ellington, Missouri, where a farmer became the first victim of 11 claimed in the state. In neighboring Illinois, half of the town of Gorham was either killed or injured and the tornado continued to pick off mining towns. Schools became a common target and dozens of children died. Farms were also ruined, alongside the homes and businesses of Princeton in Indiana before the tornado vanished.

LONDON GREAT BRITAN
January 6, 1928 **FLOOD**

Right: A flood barricade at Millbank on the River Thames, London.

In all, 14 people died when floodwater from the River Thames swept through Britain's capital—those living in basement apartments proving most vulnerable. A sudden thaw combined with a high tide put parts of London under several meters of water. Vaults at the Palace of Westminster were flooded and, for the first time in years, the moat at the Tower of London was filled. At least a dozen major works at the Tate gallery were badly damaged as was property across the city.

1928

CALBUCO CHILE
January 6, 1929 **VOLCANO**

Federico Reichert was climbing Derrumbo, a neighboring peak, when the volcanic eruption began:

"After setting out downhill at about 7 o'clock in the morning, we found ourselves faced by a strange condition. At first we had the sensation that it was raining, but very quickly found that we were mistaken. We looked up and verified the fact that it was a volcanic eruption, which in my judgement proceeded from the mountain Calbuco, situated some 9–12 miles from the spot . . . Little by little the sky was darkening more. The south cove of Lake Todos los Santos was wrapped in an impenetrable blackness . . . At 9 o'clock we reached our moored boat . . . We rowed 10 minutes and found ourselves in the dark, in the middle of a starless night. Under such conditions like blind men, we kept on rowing, anxious to gain the shore. Ordinarily this could be done in 10 minutes, but we now rowed madly for 10 hours and a half. We seemed to navigate in a vacuum. The rain of ash bathed our bodies and faces and hindered our looking upward. The situation became complicated a little later by a phenomenon no less strange. We were wrapped in the "fire of St Elmo," produced by the high electric tension. From our clothes and our flesh we gave off sparks, and our heads seemed to be surrounded by aureoles. Suddenly the lightning flashed, followed immediately by thunder. The light of the celestial discharge, however, was not enough to tear the curtain of ash and nocturnal darkness which covered everything. Simultaneously the discharges from our bodies stopped and we found ourselves again in chaos . . . Without warning we reached the shore. To orient ourselves we lit matches and debarked without difficulty. We were absolutely ignorant of the point where we arrived. At last, at 11.30, the sky began to clear and we distinguished smokily some outlines of the vicinity. To our surprise we found that we were scarcely 33 feet from the place where we had set out."

PARACUTIN VENEZUELA
February 20, 1943 **VOLCANO**

Dionisio Pulido, joint owner of the Rancho Tepacua in which Paracutin was formed remembered:

"At 4 o'clock I left my wife to set fire to a pile of branches which Demetrio and I and another . . . had gathered. I went to burn the branches when I noticed that . . . a fissure had opened, and I saw that this fissure, as I followed it with my eye, was long and passed from where I stood . . . and continued in the direction of the Cerro de Canijuata . . . Here is something new and strange, thought I, and I searched the ground for signs to see whether or not it had opened that night, but could find none . . . I set about to ignite the branches again, when I felt a thunder, the trees trembled, and I turned to speak to Paula; it was then that I saw how the hole in the ground raised and swelled itself, six and a half to eight feet high, and a kind of smoke or fine dust, which was gray like ash, began to rise, with a hiss or whistle, loud and continuous, and there was a smell of sulfur . . . I ran to see if I could save my wife and my companions and my oxen, but I could not find them . . . Then, very frightened, I mounted my mare and galloped to Paracutin, where I found my wife and son and friends waiting, fearing that I was dead and that they would never see me again. On the road to Paracutin, I had thought of my little animals, the yoke oxen, that were going to die in the flame and the smoke, but upon arriving at my house I was happy to see that they were there."

VESUVIUS ITALY
March, 1944 VOLCANO

Vesuvias has been continuously active during the last thousand years, erupting 20 times since the 18th century alone. The following pictures show some of the scenes of previous disasters. Further images can be seen on pages 37, 38, 39 and 43.

Below: *The Eruption of Vesuvius,* painted in 1777 by Jacques-Antoine Volaire.

Right: The destruction at Boscotrecase, Italy caused by the eruption of Mt Vesuvius.

Overleaf: A view of Pompeii, Italy, as it appeared in the late 19th century.

An anonymous eyewitness account of lava flows overrunning San Sebastiano on Vesuvius in March 1944:

"Since the small hours of this morning lava from Vesuvius has been slowly eating its way through the village . . . In the darkness of the night, flames, the incandescent glow from the rolling masses of lava, and above all the great lambant tongue on the mountainside overhanging all, make it indescribably awesome, but daylight deprives it of much of its terror, and the flaming monster becomes just a gradually glowing coketip . . . The progress of destruction is almost maddeningly slow. There is nothing about it like the sudden wrath of devastation by bombing . . . As it gradually filled up the backyards of houses on the village street the flow seemed to pause. Very slowly the glowing mass piled itself up against the walls with all its weight. For a while it seemed as if it would engulf the houses as they stood but then, as the weight grew, a crack would appear in the wall. As it slowly widened first one wall would fall out and then the whole house would collapse and the mass would gradually creep over it, swallowing up the debris with it."

HAWAII USA
April 1, 1946 **TSUNAMI**

Right: A Hawaiian street damaged by the tidal wave that swept the region in 1946.

Below: Bewildered residents wander among the tsunami ravaged ruins of their homes.

The largest and most devastating of tsunami waves to ever hit Hawaii occurred early on the morning of April 1, 1946. Triggered by an earthquake measuring 7.1 on the Richter Scale in the Aleutian Islands off Alaska, the waves were reported to be up to 16.5 meters (55 feet) at Pololu Valley on the Big Island.

In some areas the waves struck over half a mile inland and between the crests the 150 meter (500 feet) deep sea floor was exposed as the waves receded. It was impossible to give any prior warning for this disaster and a total of 159 tsunami related deaths resulted.

"WINTER OF TERROR"
SWITZERLAND AND AUSTRIA
1950–51 **AVALANCHE**

Right: Just one of the flood-wrecked homes in Lynmouth, Devon. The scene was likened to a World War I battlefield.

The phrase "at the mercy of the elements" is a well-known platitude. But residents of the Alps in Europe learned just what it meant during a winter which brought colossal snow falls followed by avalanche upon avalanche. Unprecedented weather conditions caused the snow that fell by the foot rather than the inch, piling up precariously before giving way to the inevitable. No European country with territory in the Alps escaped unscathed. Germany, France, Italy, and Switzerland were all visited with death and destruction. But worst hit was the centrally situated Austria. The first wave of avalanches caused mayhem and then they kept coming. Entirely random they could be only hours or, occasionally, weeks apart.

The town of Andermatt was typical. A first snow slip destroyed a military hospital, the next blocked the main road. When a third crashed across the railway line the residents were trapped. They could only wait and hope that the worst was over. It wasn't. Another avalanche came soon afterwards surging through the center of town and burying 11 people. The snow continued to fall and the avalanches carried on occurring. At the end of the winter the death toll across Europe stood at 265, with 100 of the dead killed in Austria. Forests had been wiped from mountainsides and livestock obliterated.

LYNMOUTH DEVON GREAT BRITAIN
August 16, 1952 **FLOOD**

Once it was a pretty Devon harbor typified by stone-built cottages and thatched inns, nestling beneath the hills of Exmoor. Within sight of its main street two rivers converged and bubbled down to the sea. However, after freak storms that brought heavy rain, the rivers were turned into raging torrents which rose until the creek which contained the tiny estuary could no longer hold the waters. The town was soon swamped by water clogged with debris collected on higher ground. In all, 31 people died, including three boy scouts camping by the river and a postman on his rounds. That delightful coastal resort was for years scarred by the death and destruction that occurred that day. In the aftermath of the disaster housing minister Harold MacMillan likened it to a World War I battlefield when he said it resembled "the road Ypres."

WACO USA
May 11, 1953 **TORNADO**

A massive tornado caused mayhem in Waco on a May afternoon when the horizon turned from innocent blue to ominous black. It killed 114 people, injured nearly 600 more and caused some 41 million dollars worth of damage. Almost 200 businesses were leveled, including a six-story furniture shop, the bricks of which crushed two cars and their five occupants when they tumbled into the street. A further 30 people inside the building died. Some of the survivors remained buried for more than 12 hours.

ALGERIA
September 9, 1954 **EARTHQUAKE**

Below Right: An injured man is carried away from the Algerian earthquake scene.

Far Right: Preists gaze at a demolished church in Orleansville, Algeria.

The town of Orleansville and its people were plagued by earthquakes this late summer day. No less than 70 shocks registered in 24 hours, 16 of which were violent. It was more than any community could stand. Over 1,000 people died and 36,000 were made homeless as street after street fell. Survivors had no choice but to abandon the town and seek refuge elsewhere in a country troubled by uprisings against French colonialist rule.

MADISON RIVER MONTANA USA
August 17, 1959 EARTHQUAKE

It seemed a tranquil night. A full moon shone on the waters of the Madison River while those campers still awake at the nearby campsite listened to the soothing sounds of flowing water. Just before midnight the idyllic scene was shattered by an earthquake that shook a chunk of mountain measuring 600 meters (2,000 feet) in length loose. It hurtled through the campsite killing 19 people and came to rest across the river where it became an effective dam. Water began to fill the canyon behind it submerging homes, trees, and US Highway 287. The US Corps of Engineers was sent in to alleviate the pressure on the newly made dam which they did by inserting spill channels for excess water. Earthquake Lake, as it was christened, soon stretched back to a purpose-built dam holding back the water of Hebgen Lake. It is now eight kilometers (five miles) long and 55 meters (180 feet) deep. A new road has been built along its shores, as have homes and holiday lets.

FRENCH RIVIERA PROVENCE FRANCE
December 3, 1959 FLOOD

When storm waters cracked the Malpasset dam in France's fashionable south, the lengthening fractures at the base were viewed with curiosity rather than alarm. It was two days before local residents appreciated the seriousness of the situation, when the dam gave way and unleashed a wall of water on the town of Frejus. It took only moments for the water to rush down a valley, taking with it houses, farms, a power station, and a train with passengers inside. The water, by now mixed with boulders, trees, and other debris, covered 25 square kilometers (10 square miles).

1959

AGADIR MOROCCO
March 1, 1960 EARTHQUAKE

An earthquake lasting just 15 seconds followed by a tsunami and a rash of blazes was sufficient to kill more than a third of the city's population, some 12,000 people. Among the dead were foreign tourists. Ancient quarters of the city were wiped out and three quarters of the new hotels and apartments built for an infant tourist trade were flattened. When he saw the devastation Crown Prince Moulay Hassan decided to cut all losses by building an entirely new city. "The old one has ceased to exist," he declared. The Prince, who became king less than a year afterwards, was as good as his word and created a tourists' paradise that has long aided the country's economy.

Above: The Agadir earthquake literally reduced much of the city to rubble as well as killing some 12,000 inhabitants.

CHILE
May 22, 1960 **EARTHQUAKE**

Above: An aerial view of earthquake damage on the waterfront in southern Chile.

Over 2,000 people were killed and ten times that many were left homeless after the world's worst earthquake rocked southern Chile. It measured 9.5 on the scale, the strongest yet recorded, rupturing the sea bed for about 850 kilometers (525 miles). The epicenter was off the coast and consequently a tsunami more than nine meters (30 feet) in height tore along the shore, consuming numerous fishing villages in its path. Damage was not confined to Chile alone. The tsunami caused 61 deaths and 75 million dollars worth of damage in Hawaii and 138 deaths and 50 millions dollars worth of damage in Japan, which was 13,000 kilometers (8,000 miles) from the source. There were 32 dead in the Philippines and 500,000 dollars worth of damage was done along the west coast of the United States. In addition to the tsunami, the people of Chile had to contend with landslides. These falls of rocks and mud blocked rivers and lakes and perpetuated the danger of flooding. Probably due to the earthquake, the Puyehue volcano erupted two days following.

Left: That these Chilean houses are standing at all is a miracle after an earthquake measuring 9.5 on the Richter Scale.

Below Left: Children play among the wreckage of their city. Note the tension cracks in the road.

NEVADA HUASCARAN PERU
January 10, 1962 AVALANCHE

History's worst avalanche disaster devastated everything in its 16 kilometer (10 mile) path. It took just seven minutes for the mass of ice that dislodged itself from a melting glacier somewhere near the summit of Nevada Huscaran to complete its descent. By the time it came to a halt the three million ton avalanche had accrued mud, rock, trees, livestock, top soil, and homes. The debris covered an enormous area.

Standing at more than 6,700 meters (22,000 feet) high, Huscaran is the second highest mountain in the Andes. Villages were warned about the impending disaster by the mighty crash of the moving ice but there was nothing they could do to escape its path. The casualties included some 4,000 residents of nine mountain villages in Peru and 10,000 cattle, sheep, and goats.

VAIONT DAM ALPS ITALY
October 9, 1963 FLOOD

The fall of 1963 was one of the wettest on record in the Italian Alps. By the end of September the earth was so saturated that the lubricating effect on mountain soil and scree was causing occasional mini-landslides. Beneath the spectacular ridge of 1,800 meter (6,000 feet) Mount Toc, engineers on the Vaiont Dam hydro-electric power project noted these subtle signs of instability and on October 8, they issued a warning to all walkers and anglers, urging them to keep away until conditions improved. The concern was that a landslip into the dam might produce a wave big enough to sweep away anyone standing on the edge. This foresight was absolutely spot on. It was the scale of the danger which failed to register.

The v-shaped dam, rising 265 meters (828 feet) above the Piave River, was one of five in the area commissioned by Italy's state-run electricity generator to provide cheap and efficient energy. When opened in 1960 it was the third-largest concrete dam in the world and the pride of the country's civil engineering industry. It's two great advantages lay in its pollution-free operation and an ability to meet surges in power demand by adjusting the massive generating turbines fitted in tunnels at the foot of the structure. If demand was high, these would be fully opened—directing millions of gallons of highly-pressured water through the turbines to produce maximum output. During slack periods, several could be closed to put the dam in "tick-over" mode.

At about 10.45 pm on the night of October 9, an automatic seismic recorder placed on Mount Toc registered an earth tremor. It was a strong signal, though it would not have been expected to cause a problem on its own. The Vaiont monitoring team logged it as just another landslip. In the valley below, in the villages of Longarone, Fae, Pirago, Codissago, and Castellavazzo, the lights gradually went out as residents turned in to bed.

Later, one scientist would liken the effect of the tremor to a child holding an upturned bucket of compressed wet sand over a beach. Although the sand is lubricated, it sticks in place. But if the bucket is shaken that stability is lost and the sand pours out. So it was with Vaiont.

At 11.15 pm the continual falling and sliding of rocks and earth triggered by the initial tremor turned into one, great, unstoppable landslip. Some locals later likened it to the sound of rolling thunder, but with a deeper and more sinister quality. It was distinctive enough for some to believe immediately that the dam had burst and run with their children into the open air. In fact, the thousands of tons of collapsing rubble had set up a huge shockwave which over-topped the wall of the dam. This

Above: Flood survivors survey the damage in the Italian village of Longarone after flood waters from the Vaiont Dam roared through the village, destroying most of it and killing over 2,000 people.

foaming, gray-brown tide of death crashed through the valley below, sweeping away houses, roads, telephones, and power lines. At least 80 per cent of Longarone was destroyed at a stroke; every citizen of Fae and Pirago was drowned and both Codissago and Castellavazzo lost half their populations. Only those who lived in isolated houses or hamlets above the valley floor escaped with their lives.

It was, observed one government minister, a disaster of biblical proportions—a scene reminiscent of Pompeii before the excavations began. Relief workers found hundred upon hundred of bodies bobbing together in pools of floodwater; others had to be disentangled from uprooted trees and scrub. The dead were sprayed with disinfectant to reduce the risk of disease and laid out in lines ready for mass burial. Identification was impossible in many cases. And though the official death toll was put at 1,189, later estimates suggested it was roughly three times larger. The horrible truth is that thousands of bodies were never found.

The lessons of Vaiont were quickly learned. The mistake made by dam constructors was to conduct a woefully inadequate analysis of the surrounding natural geology and to believe that plugs of reinforced concrete would be enough to shore up the fissures and cracks created by landslides in previous years. The reality was that the steep, unstable sides of the dam were simply not strong enough to cope with the weight of water within. There was no argument when the Italian government ruled that the dam should be permanently closed.

Above: Debris and damaged buildings are all that remain of the Italian village.

Left: Survivors standing over some belongings left after the Vaiont Dam disaster.

PRINCE WILLIAM SOUND ALASKA
March 27, 1964 **EARTHQUAKE**

One of the most severe earthquakes to hit North America occurred in the early hours of this Good Friday, causing a mighty tsunami which swept up the Alaskan coastline. It measured 9.2 on the Richter Scale, and its three minutes of violent shaking brought about a massive movement of earth. The capital, Anchorage, was 190 kilometers (120 miles) from the epicenter but still sustained extensive damage.

Buildings collapsed and tilted at crazy angles. Water and gas mains, electricity supplies, sewers, and telephone wires were severed. And the widespread disruption was compounded by large and devastating landslides.

The loss of life was remarkably small, only 131 died following the quake, which was millions of times more powerful than the bomb which fell on Hiroshima in 1945.

Most were killed in the powerful sweep of the tsunami. Its effect was felt not only in the Bay of Alaska and along the west coast of America, it was even witnessed through wave movements as far south as Cuba and Puerto Rico.

Afterwards it was estimated that 90,000 square kilometers (35,000 square miles) had been permanantly lifted and that the sea bed between Kodiak and Montague Islands had risen about 15 meters (50 feet).

ABERFAN SOUTH WALES
October 21, 1966 **LANDSLIP**

Right: Destraught villagers pick through the remains of Pantglas Junior School, Aberfan. Rescue workers faced the terrible knowledge that their own children were in the school.

Ten year old Eryl Mai Jones was troubled by the vivid dreams which haunted her sleep the previous night.

"I dreamed I went to school and there was no school there. Something black had come down over it," she explained to her mother.

The following day she braved the drizzle to go to Pantglas Junior School as usual, sang "All Things Bright and Beautiful" in assembly, and doubtless chatted and joked with her friends—until her dream turned to grim reality. A 180 meter (600 feet) high heap of coal waste perched above the village of Aberfan was made unstable by heavy rain. With a thundering, vibrating roar the black heap shifted then slid down the hill.

A 15 meter (50 feet) wide wall comprising two million tons of black slurry traveled at about 50 kilometers per hour (30 miles per hour),

flattening a farmhouse before enveloping the Victorian one-story school. It was all over in a matter of minutes. Afterward, survivors told how children and teachers alike were rooted to the spot in terror. Even those with enough presence of mind to dive under desks or make for the door were not guaranteed survival.

Rescuers were quickly on the scene, including miners from the colliery at Methyr Tydfil. They were hampered both by two fractured water pipes that were gushing over the area and the trauma of digging out the bodies of small children, sometimes their own.

Of the 126 children at school that day only ten survived.

Eryl Mai Jones was not alone in her psychic experience. Afterwards there were numerous reports of people who had been overcome with foreboding in the days and hours before the tragedy with visions of billowing black clouds and screaming children.

But there was nothing supernatural about the disaster that killed 29 adults and 116 children. This, the No. 7 tip, which had been built over a natural spring, grew so large it could no longer contain itself. However, the National Coal Board responsible for mine workings refused to accept responsibility for the disaster. Indeed, the coal board claimed £150,000 from the £2.5 million disaster fund, boosted by donations from across the world, to pay for the removal of similar waste tips. Furious Aberfan residents were told that, unless the fund contributed to costs, some of the tips could be left in place and landscaped, thus risking a similar disaster occurring again. The sum was repaid by the British government over 30 years after the disaster.

The town of Aberfan was robbed of a generation. Survivors, perhaps bore the heaviest burden.

"We hung about on a farm and had to grow up very quickly. There was no one else to play with. We didn't do what other kids do; there weren't enough of us left to form a football side," remembers Jeff Edwards who was trapped by a collapsed radiator for an hour and a half. "The little girl next to me was dead and her head was on my shoulder."

"We didn't go out to play for a long time, because those who'd lost their own children couldn't bear to see us. We all knew what they were feeling and we felt guilty about being alive," explains Gaynor Madgwick, who was likewise both crushed and saved by a radiator.

Janett Smart recalls the harsh reality of survival. "We were always told we were lucky to be alive. I suppose everybody in the village was so badly affected that nobody had the time to give us any sympathy."

According to Gerald Kirwan there was a conspiracy of silence. "What happened in Aberfan that day was the dark little secret when we were young and it still is. We knew we must not speak out. We have been quiet for the sake of the other people, those who lost children and those who did not want to hear about what happened, especially from the mouths of their own children."

It was only some 30 years after the disaster that some of the survivors felt able to compare notes about their experience. Most missed huge chunks of schooling following the slurry fall, became afraid of the dark, could picture victims clearly in their mind's eye, and long pondered the random nature of survival, on why they had lived when others died.

FLORENCE ITALY
November 5, 1966 **FLOOD**

A nation's rich heritage was left sodden and coated in green slime when 40 hours of rain drenched Europe. Two thirds of Florence, the cultural capital of Italy, was under two meters (six feet) of water after the River Arno burst its banks. The force of the rising waters was such that the bronze "Door of Paradise" from the Duomo was swept away.

The famous Uffizi Gallery had a massive clean-up operation on its hands, as did the National Library, where thousands of books were soaked. Equipment usually used to dry tobacco leaves was rushed in to assist. Salvage work, which was remarkably successful, rectified some of the damage. Still, experts rated the cost of the disaster as at least £58 million. There was a human cost, too. Nearly 200 people in Italy and the surrounding countries affected by the rogue weather perished.

Below Left: People gaze from windows at wrecked cars in a water-logged street in Florence, following the devastating flood of November 1966, during which the water of the Arno rose as high as six meters (20 feet), submerging sculpture, paintings, mosaics, and manuscripts in the city's libraries.

Far Left: A wrecked car is left by Michaelangelo's *David* **in Florence.**

Above Left: The ruins of Ponte Vecchio, Florence. Note the collection of debris that has accumulated, showing the height that the river reached.

Middle Left: Debris floats in a flooded Florentine piazza.

Below Left: A collapsed road by the river in Florence.

Overleaf: A man paddles a small boat among wrecked cars on a waterlogged street.

EAST PAKISTAN
November 18, 1970 **CYCLONE**

Above: Survivors file past the body of a victim of the East Pakistan tsunami.

Right: A steamer ship tossed onto a field by the raging waters which accompanied a devastating cyclone. The cyclone hit much of the coast of East Pakistan.

Delta dwellers—not for the first time—were helpless victims when a typhoon in the company of a tsunami visited the region around the Dhaka. As many as 150,000 perished, killed as they slept—for the terror struck at around midnight. Soldier Ali Husain, 25, explained that he owed his life to a stoutly rooted tree, "I caught hold of a palm tree and hung on until the waters went down around dawn."

MANAGUA NICARAGUA
December 25, 1972 **EARTHQUAKE**

While the Christmas Day theme is usually one of "peace on earth" the tradition was crushed in the rubble after an earthquake razed two thirds of the capital city of Nicaragua. As many as 10,000 died either directly in the earthquake or in fires that broke out afterwards. Howard Hughes, the reclusive millionaire, was one of 3,000 Americans left counting their blessings after surviving the trauma.

Below Left: An aerial view of damage caused by the Nicaraguan earthquake that leveled two thirds of the capital city on Christmas Day 1972.

Bottom Left: A woman holds onto an artificial Christmas tree amid the earthquake devastation in her neighborhood.

WICHITA FALLS USA
April 10, 1979 **TORNADO**

Instinct told the residents of Wichita Falls to take to their cars when a tornado measuring one and a half kilometers (one mile) wide visited their town. Alarmed by the different colored clouds spinning in all directions, residents knew the twister would be with them imminently. Alas, their instinct was wrong. Of 42 deaths that day in Wichita Falls, 25 of them were linked to the use of cars. More than half of those seriously injured were also in cars. Witness Joel Manes recalled: "It was only a mile or a mile and a half wide but when it is only two miles away it was huge. I can still hear it now. The little clouds that were shooting toward it were being shipped upward into the tornado and power lines were sparking and stuff was flying everywhere."

It was one of 13 tornadoes to touch down that day in Texas and Oklahoma and remains one of the most damaging tornadoes in American history.

Mt St HELENS
WASHINGTON USA
May 18, 1980 **VOLCANO**

Right: Voluminous plumes of volcanic ash and rock blast from the side of Mt St Helens in July 1980.

This giant of the Cascade Range in south west Washington, which had been sleeping since 1857, began to roar again from March 1980, quietly at first and then with ever greater velocity. There were earthquakes, too, proof that the planet's mantle was ready to snap.

St Helens collapsed then exploded, blasting ash with a temperature of 300 degrees centigrade (572 degrees fahrenheit) some 2 kilometers (one and a half miles) into the air. Similar to the disaster at Mt Pelée in 1902, St Helen's was tagged a *nuée ardente*—or glowing cloud—which denotes a particularly violent eruption. Fortunately, the authorities, on the advice of vulcanologists, had closed off the area. Still, more than 60 people died and all wildlife in an area measuring some 180 square kilometers (70 square miles) was destroyed. Ash and debris was spread still further.

The volcano unleashed an avalance and millions of tons of snow was shifted at speeds of 400 kilometres per hour (250 miles per hour).

Although it continues to belch steam and ash intermittently, St Helens has become a Mecca for vulcanologists and data collected on the eruption fills volumes. The eruption of 1980 left it some 400 meters (1,300 feet) shorter in stature.

Left and Above: Various stages of the eruption of Mt St Helens.

NEVADO DEL RUIZ COLOMBIA
November 13, 1985 VOLCANO

It was no surprise when Colombia's Nevado del Ruiz began belching fire that November night. Just two months before, volcanic activity had sent a mudslide down its north eastern side and the murmurings of the mountain were sufficient to alarm geologists who warned the Colombian government of possible hazards ahead. Nothing was done to evacuate the town of Armero, 45 kilometers (28 miles) from the crater and towns-folk were not unduly alarmed.

As the volcano sparked, hot ashes fell on the local glacier in great quantities. Both the glacier and the snow around it began to melt and formed a fast-moving river heading downhill, gathering debris and further black ash *en route*. By the time it reached Armero it was a viscous muddy blanket about four meters (13 feet) deep that engulfed everything in its path. The mud flows killed 22,000, about 90 per cent of the local population.

MOUNT PINATUBO PHILIPPINES
June 15, 1991 VOLCANO

Right: The barren scene of the aftermath of Pinatubo's unexpected eruption—the Philippine hills are covered with volcanic ash.

About 88 kilometers (55 miles) north of Manila stands Mount Pinatubo, a gentle giant that had not puffed so much as a wisp of smoke for 600 years. The summer of 1991 changed all of that when it threw millions of tons of ash and tephra some 15,000 meters (50,000 feet) into the air. Tropical rains turned the volcanic ash to mud and there were catastrophic landslides in the wake of the explosions. The eruption ejected huge quantities of sulfur-rich clouds into the atmosphere which led to global cooling for months afterwards.

Fear of this major volcanic explosion was countered by rumors that, along with lava and tehpra, diamonds were being thrown out by the mountain. Alas for the local population, the gems were in fact worthless quartz crystals.

It is thought that 550 people died in the eruption and its aftermath. About 650,000 people lost their livelihood, with 100,000 hectares (50,000 acres) smothered and singed. The mountain, which erupted again in August 1992, now stands at 1,750 meters (5,770 feet) high.

LOS ANGELES CALIFORNIA USA
January 17, 1994 **EARTHQUAKE**

Right: An aerial view of the "Stanford Hill" escarpment, near Los Angeles formed by an earthquake. This region is one of the many worldwide that are particularly at risk from earthquakes. Locals live in constant dread of "the big one."

Since the San Francisco earthquake of 1906, the population of California has been awaiting "the big one." The mighty earth movement that brought San Francisco to its knees wreaked havoc and, given an increase in population and urban sprawl, if a tremor of the same strength occurred today the death toll would soar.

When an earthquake measuring 6.7 on the Richter scale rocked Los Angeles it brought down three flyovers and undermined thousands of homes and businesses, which were subsequently declared unsafe. Yet, by common consent, this was not the cataclysmic event for which everyone had been holding their breath. Moderate rather than large, it was merely one of numerous earthquakes that shake the region regularly.

It was 4.30 am when the earthquake struck at Northridge in northern Los Angeles. In all, 57 people were killed and more than 1,500 injured. Fires raged after being triggered by the earthquake, and, in common with other earthquakes, electricity, gas, and water supplies were disrupted and thousands of people were left homeless.

Given the time it occurred, the residents of San Fernando Valley where the quake happened breathed a sigh of relief. Buildings that collapsed were empty when just six hours later they might have been full. Masonry fell onto deserted roads that would soon be jammed with cars. These were exceptionally strong ground earth motions, after all.

It was the second time in 23 years that the region, which lies some 100 kilometers (60 miles) from the San Andreas fault, had been shaken by a sizeable earthquake. The epicenters were just 32 kilometers (20 miles) apart. In 1971, the death toll was 58 and 2,000 were injured. On October 17, 1989 the Loma Prieta earthquake south of San Francisco, during which a one and a half kilometer (one mile) stretch of the Nimitz freeway crashed down on West Oakland, was greater in magnitude than that at Northridge but caused less damage.

The awareness of earthquake danger is reflected in the preparation that major cities and residents of the region take.

Los Angeles has a well-rehearsed earthquake drill that swings easily into action. Large amounts of public money have been pumped into the fire and rescue services allowing for plenty of manpower and up-to-date equipment. Its chiefs, along with the mayor, police supremos, and top level bureaucrats, are coached to operate out of a quake-proof center below City Hall. Building codes are stringent, although the 1994 earthquake revealed that many older buildings had not been brought into line.

Above: Three views of the destruction caused by tremors in the Los Angeles district.

Right: A demolished building on Olympic Boulevard in Los Angeles, after the January 17, earthquake.

KOBE JAPAN
January 17, 1995 EARTHQUAKE

Above: Automobiles on a street along the waterfront submerged in water after the 1995 earthquake in Kobe, Honshu, Japan.

Right: The Kobe earthquake, which measured 7.2 on the Richter Scale, caused widespread suffering and massive destruction of property as can be seen in this photograph.

The residents of Tokyo have always been well acquainted with the risks posed by earthquakes. Rumbles in the region are frequent and most of the prediction and monitoring efforts are centered there. The folk of Kobe, some 450 kilometers (280 miles) distant, were not as familiar with the threat. Until the dawn of that January day they paid little heed to the possibility of destruction by earthquake, the last one to strike there being as long ago as 1916, and that one was not considered major.

All that changed in just 20 seconds when Kobe and the neighboring industrial centers of Osaka and Kyoto were laid waste by a tremor that measured 7.2 on the Richter scale. Its focus was 20 kilometers (12.5 miles) under Awaji in the Inland Sea. The death toll topped 5,000.

Kobe was hardest hit. It was alight with the eruption of fires across the city. Power lines were felled in the streets. Water mains became fountains, noxious gas from ruptured pipes filled the air. Tense survivors lit their cigarettes, blithely unaware of the hazard.

The earthquake was the worst to hit Japan for almost 50 years. For the first time, some of the engineering designed to counter the effects of earthquakes, into which the Japanese had sunk millions of dollars, was put to the test. Some pieces were found wanting. Allegedly earthquake proof buildings and bridge supports defied their maker's recommendations by fracturing. Motorways which cost 50 per cent more than those in other countries were wrecked. This is partly due to the strong vertical motion of the earthquake but adequately illustrates how difficult it is to defend against natural disasters.

Dr Michael Miller, dean of the Kobe Institute, said: "It was like being in a huge jelly. The building shook and everything that was not bolted down either fell over, slipped across the floors, or fell off the wall. The whole of Kobe exploded in flames."

Survivors gathered in shelters picked from the least damaged buildings. But of course there was no fresh water, no electricity, no comforts amid the rubble. And the hazards were far from over. There were powerful aftershocks which continued for days. Gregory Fremont-Barnes, a lecturer in European history at the Kobe Institute, afterwards experienced the syndrome of survivors "guilt." "With each aftershock—frequent and frightening, they make a rolling sound like thunder and raise your heart-rate to the point that you can feel the pressure of blood pumping in your chest—there is the feeling that we don't deserve to have been so lucky."

If the Japanese people were alarmed by the earthquake, their shock turned to horror at the inadequate response of the government. It took

the prime minister Tomiichi Murayama a week to declare the area a disaster zone. Justifying his inaction, Mr Murayama said: "It was the first time this kind of thing has happened." Even the most casual observer would know this not to be true.

French doctors were unable to assist because they did not hold the correct medical licences. Rescuers loitered outside collapsed buildings waiting for official permission to look for survivors inside. When the army finally arrived it failed to clear the streets for access by the emergency services. The catalog of failures goes on and on.

There was one beacon of encouragement shining through the wreckage. Despite the unsteady ground, the ancient Toji Temple remained standing. Only two of Japan's 500 wooden pagodas built in the region of 1,400 years ago have succumbed to the power of earthquakes.

JARRELL TEXAS USA
May 28, 1997 **TORNADO**

It took the twister just five minutes to sweep through town. In its wake it left death and destruction reminiscent of a war zone. Tragically, 32 people died in Jarrell as the tornado—one of eight to hit Texas that day—scythed a path more than one and a half kilometers (one mile) long and 730 meters (2,400 feet) wide. Those who died were in cars, in the 50 or more houses that were razed, or were ranch workers caught outdoors with no protection. Telegraph poles in the vicinity were snapped like reeds. One survivor from the 400-strong community, Max Johnson, said: "It was like a big vacuum that sucked everything up."

Left: Buildings in Kobe, Japan, which were designed to rigorous standards to survive the onslaught of a major earthquake, completely failed to fulfill the promise of architects and engineers.

THREDBO AUSTRALIA
July 30, 1997 **LANDSLIDE**

Hope survives until the last piece of landslide debris has been cleared. That's the philosophy of rescue teams everywhere, not least because it boosts their own morale as well as everybody else's. And so it was with the rescuers working at Thredbo in Australia.

But many must have had doubts after a landslide brought boulders, soil, and trees 200 meters (650 feet) down a slope in the Snowy Mountains and flattened two ski-lodges. In all, 20 people—17 Australians, two Americans, and a New Zealander—were buried in the rubble.

The landslip happened just before midnight on Wednesday. After the rescuers were given the go-ahead they sifted painstakingly through the timber struts that were once a building, and mud that was once part of a mountain. Sniffer dogs were at work and other equipment included thermal imagers which reflect body heat and acoustic detectors to pick up sounds or vibrations.

There was a constant threat of further landslips as the mountain remained unstable. To anxious on-lookers it was a painfully slow process. It felt the same for fireman Ewan Diver whose brother Stewart and sister-in-law Sally were among those trapped.

Thursday turned into Friday and there was still no sign of life coming from beneath the tangled heap. Work continued into the early hours of Saturday in the face of freezing temperatures by rescue workers who by now admitted their chances of finding anyone alive were "infinitesimally small."

Suddenly, before dawn, there was a sound. Sydney fireman and rescue specialist Steve Hirst could barely believe his ears. Immediately he silenced the drilling machinery nearby and called out. "Rescue team working overhead, can anyone hear me?"

"Yeah, I can hear you," came the reply. It was 31-year-old ski-instructor Stewart Diver. Trapped under ten meters (35 feet) of rubble, suffering from frostbite and hypothermia, he was still, against all odds, alive. "It's freezing in here . . . get me a blanket," Diver called.

Spirits soared but the task of getting Diver out alive was still a monumental one. It was seven hours before the rescuers created a hole through which to hold Diver's hand. After that they were able to pass down a torch, a glucose drip, and a pipe which blew warm air from a generator over Diver's cold body. Paramedics stayed at the scene giving words of encouragement despite the threat of further slips.

The trapped man's courage astounded those around him. He was compelled to lie immobile while heavy machinery attacked two slabs of concrete which were pinning him down.

Over 12 hours after Diver was discovered he was lifted out of the chamber that so nearly became his tomb. When he arrived at hospital in Canberra doctors were amazed that the injuries he suffered bodily during 50 hours of incarceration were comparatively slight. He had escaped serious hypothermia probably with protection from the rubble.

But joy at his survival was tempered with grief for the rest of those buried who perished, including his wife Sally. He told rescuers how a tide of mud and water swept her from his arms.

ASSISI ITALY
September 26, 1997 EARTHQUAKE

St Francis of Assisi (1182–1226), the friend of the animals who sold all his worldly possessions in order to devote himself to God, has been an inspiration to generations.

Tucked into the Umbrian hills, his home town of Assisi became famous on the strength of his reputation. Visitors and pilgrims flocked there, enchanted by the Basilica of San Francesco with its frescoes by Giotti and others. In the crypt of the Basilica, which was founded two years after the death of the saint and completed in 1253, lies the body of St Francis. Soon afterward the gothic Basilisca of Santa Chiara was constructed and it houses the body of St Clare who, with St Francis, founded the Order of the Poor Clares. As if these two landmarks were not enough, there's also the Cathedral of San Rufino with its impressive Romanesque edifice.

The population of 25,000 was rightly proud of this gem of a town. And their horror when an earthquake caused hideous damage to key buildings was shared by the rest of the world. The Basilica where the saint had rested peacefully for centuries was part-collapsed. Among the debris were the shattered fragments of Giotti's handiwork. Just 11 people died which made it fairly harmless in earthquake terms, but it happened in a country surprised by the seismic activity that claimed so much of its heritage. The earthquake measured less than five on the Richter Scale but it was in an area where nothing has been built to withstand ground movement. The aftershocks—as potent as the main shock—rippled through the region for months afterward, causing further damage and terror. A month after the main shock a rumble brought the bell tower of the Umbrian town of Foligno crashing down into the square where once St Francis renounced all his material goods.

The homeless—there were more than 10,000 of them—were housed in tents before being transferred to metallic mobile homes. Many were forced to leave all their worldly possessions in homes deemed too dangerous to enter. Their misery was compounded when they saw bulldozers finish the job started by the earthquake of flattening their homes. It was then a case of waiting until new homes were built before life could continue and memories of the trauma could begin to recede.

PAPAU NEW GUINEA
July 17, 1998 TSUNAMI

To helpless witnesses, it seemed that the sea rose up in anger and swallowed the side of an island. Evening was falling when the first of three giant waves loomed, caused by a submarine earthquake 29 kilometers (18 miles) out to sea that measured at least seven on the Richter Scale.

The first warning for residents of the beachfront settlements on Papua New Guinea's north west coast was a shaking beneath their feet as the tremor rumbled. Next, there was a roar similar to that of a jet fighter. Then the three tsunamis came up out of the water, the last and biggest measuring nine meters (30 feet) in height.

Flimsy housing was instantly turned into driftwood. The occupants were swept into the Sissano lagoon that lays behind the seven villages that were ripped to pieces. Beyond that there is only inhospitable jungle and swamp.

Rescue workers retrieved bodies from sea, swamp, and jungle. Survivors were dug out of the sand and rubble. Some who escaped death in the waves and sought refuge in the mangroves undoubtedly perished for lack of fresh water and food before they were discovered. Australia mounted a relief operation but found difficulties in reaching the remote area, which was soon running short of supplies. Nevertheless, there were some high notes. A nun at the local Catholic mission said: "They picked up a woman hanging onto a canoe for 18 hours with a broken leg and they also dug out a child half buried that was still alive."

The death toll amounted to about 4,000, about half of the local population.

BANGLADESH
July 20, 1998 FLOOD

Right: This aerial view taken by a reconnaissance aircraft shows a mosque in Bangladesh flooded by the waters of the Ganges, which broke its banks on July 20, 1998.

Eight million people were made homeless when monsoon rains swelled the Ganges to hitherto unimagined heights. Many areas were condemned to stay under water for two months and some areas were cut off with rapidly dwindling supplies as the currents in the flood waters proved too treacherous to cross. Lessons were suspended at more than 13,300 schools, some of which were damaged by the rising waters while others became shelters for the homeless. Cattle that escaped death in the floods were then struck down with cattle fever. Thousands died as it proved impossible to reach and treat the stricken animals and the future livelihood of millions was put in jeopardy.

After the flood receded, the World Health Organization reported that as many as 20 million people in the region would suffer from related diseases, chiefly diarrhea, skin problems, dysentery, breathing difficulties, malaria, and ear and eye infections.

CENTRAL AMERICA
October 29, 1998 **HURRICANE**

In October 1998, the fourth most powerful Caribbean hurricane of the 20th century built itself into a 290 kilometer per hour (180 mile per hour) fury and began tracking across the western Atlantic toward the coast of Central America. By the time its dreadful work was complete, Hurricane Mitch had claimed well over 10,000 lives and left two million people homeless in Honduras, Belize, Nicaragua, and Mexico. In the case of Honduras, officials estimated that around 60 per cent of the nation's infrastructure was destroyed within the space of a few hours.

The high winds were bad enough, but they were not the storm's deadliest feature. When it made landfall it instantly decreased in intensity (a common phenomena given that hurricanes feed off the warmth and moisture of the sea's surface) and was downgraded by tracking stations to "tropical storm" status. This technicality mattered little considering Mitch's new destructive element. The winds interacted with cool, moisture-laden air across the region's mountains to create a five-day cloudburst. In some areas it was estimated that 65 centimeters (25 inches) of rain fell inside 24 hours—the equivalent of a year's rainfall in London. The effect of such volumes of water was predictably catastrophic and for hundreds of poor, rural communities there was nowhere to run.

Swollen rivers burst their banks, churned and gouged out rocks and rubble, and scythed across thousands of square miles. Bridges, roads, telecommunications, houses, and public buildings were swept away; the wreckage launched like deadly floating missiles against other structures downstream. In some areas the initial torrent subsided to leave entire villages buried beneath nine meters (30 feet) of mud and silt, their inhabitants sucked into oblivion. For those who survived to tell the tale, and the rescue workers later tasked with removing hundreds of rotting corpses from the mud-swamps, the horror of those days will haunt them forever.

One of the worst-affected areas lay beneath the crater lake of the Casita volcano, 80 kilometers (50 miles) north west of the Nicaraguan capital Managua. Here, some 1,500 people were buried alive when a section of the crater wall collapsed and a saturated landslide engulfed the villages of El Porvenir, Versalles, Rolando Rodriguez, and Santa Narcisa. Rescue workers flown in on military helicopters on November 1, found 82 square kilometers (32 square miles) of the land buried beneath mud. One observer recalled seeing the limbs or bodies of the dead protruding every ten meters (32 feet) across the entire area.

One resident, Francisco Manuel Pineda, had left his home in El Porvenir early on Friday October 29, to buy medicine for his family. When he returned 48 hours later he found his house gone and no sign

Left: The Bangladesh flood of 1998 inundated the farmland that is so vital to the area's economy. Food was scarce in the wake of the disaster and disease became increasingly difficult to control. It may take many years before the region fully recovers.

of his father, mother, brothers, sisters, or sons. Survivors told him they had only the briefest of warnings. "It was raining torrentially," Mr Pineda told one interviewer. "They heard a sound like a fleet of helicopters and within minutes an avalanche of mud, tree trunks, and rocks wiped out everything."

At one stage in the aftermath of the disaster, charities and government aid organizations were revising the scale of the required relief operation every few hours. The International Red Cross announced it was tripling the target of its hurricane appeal fund to more than 7 million dollars. The Honduran President, Carlos Flores, said that his country had "receded many years" in terms of its national development and that the republic's capital, Tegucigalpa, was in a "precarious condition." In Nicaragua, President Amoldo Aleman declared three days of national mourning and conceded that the final death toll would never be known.

Later analysis of Mitch's progress showed that its most unusual feature lay in its geographical course. Atlantic and Caribbean hurricanes usually track in a clockwise curve before petering out in mid-Atlantic. For reasons still unclear, Mitch headed due west for its cataclysmic appointment with the people of central America. In looking for historical comparisons, some observers have already drawn possible parallels with the sudden abandonment of lowland Mayan villages in the tenth century AD, while those on higher ground apparently continued to flourish. This massive depopulation would be consistent with the effects of mass-flooding.

AREMENIA COLOMBIA
January 25, 1999 **EARTHQUAKE**

The death toll caused by an earthquake depends not so much on the strength of the tremor but rather on when and where it occurs. An urban center, for example, is particularly vulnerable to the collapse of high buildings, yet outside working hours may be comparatively sparsely populated. Sadly for the west Colombian cities of Armenia and Pereira, the earthquake of Monday January 25, 1999 struck at 1.19 pm as thousands of office employees sat inside at their desks or took lunch in packed downtown restaurants. Many would have had just long enough to realize what was happening before their escape routes were cut off in a roar of crumbling masonry. Given the ponderous nature of the subsequent rescue operation, those who died instantly were in some ways fortunate.

The Guadalajara restaurant in central Armenia illustrates the point. When the first tremors were felt it was frantically busy and latecomers were queuing outside for a table. Five minutes later the four-story building was barely three meters (nine feet) high, its walls and floors collapsing neatly on top of each other "like a grotesque club sandwich," as one observer put it. Rescue workers took almost 48 hours to dig their way down to the ground floor, by which time all 26 people trapped there were dead. There were heart-rending scenes as friends and relatives gathered to watch the bodies being dug out. Mingled with feelings of intense shock and grief was a sense among survivors that it could so easily have been them. One woman, Nellie Cebolla Lopez, wept uncontrollably as she saw the corpse of her sister Gloria manhandled to the surface. "We always came for lunch here, my sister and I," she said, "but on Monday I had something to do at the house and I left her outside the restaurant for lunch. I never saw her again, until now." Later the authorities confirmed that 40 per cent of Armenia's buildings had been destroyed.

The quake, measuring 6.0 on the Richter scale of 10, was the worst to hit Colombia for 16 years. Seismic activity is not unusual in the Andes but it generally occurs so deep underground that it poses no threat. This tremor was extremely shallow—barely 32 kilometers (20 miles) below the earth's surface—and set off scores of aftershocks ranging up to 5.6 on the Richter scale. The result was to bring down buildings in five provinces and even 160 kilometers (100 miles) away in the capital, Bogota, several skyscrapers swayed as a result of the ground vibration. Across this economically crucial coffee-growing area there were scenes of devastation; fractured gas mains spouting flames, fires raging through demolished buildings, landslides blocking roads, useless telephone wires grounded, and twisted water and electricity mains cut. An estimated 200,000 people left homeless. Worse, the government's emergency aid operation didn't so much swing as stutter into action.

The problem didn't lie in a lack of aid. Foreign governments and international charities such as the Red Cross reacted as quickly as could be reasonably expected. The danger was that essentials such as food, medical supplies, blankets, and—most importantly—water were not being effectively distributed to those most in need. Inevitably, starving and thirsty people took matters into their own hands; looting and ransacking supermarkets in Armenia and attacking the city's Red Cross headquarters with machetes and clubs. In an attempt to restore order, the country's President Andres Pastrana ordered 4,000 troops onto the streets and imposed a dawn to dusk curfew. "The magnitude of this tragedy exceeds all initial calculations," he told the nation in a televised address. "I will not rest until I see our emergency plan working effectively."

Government aides admitted the distribution system was in chaos. "We don't have 600 or 700 state officials to bring aid out to the communities," said Fernando Medellin, the director of Colombia's Solidarity Network organization. "The only way is for residents and officials to come to a warehouse and get it." By now the international media had latched on to the shambolic relief operation and was beaming live pictures around the world. At one police operations center in a still-habitable Armenian school, officers sat guarding a mountain of clothes, food, and bottled water. Why weren't they distributing it? They replied that they had received no orders. Their camp commandant was nowhere to be found.

Within five days of the earthquake, the death toll was 881 and rising. Around 3,550 people had been injured and thousands more faced a fast-developing risk of disease. Mortuaries were hopelessly overwhelmed and across the main urban centers there was soon the familiar sight of parked refrigerated delivery lorries, their engines running, packed with a cargo of human corpses. It was more than a month before the situation stabilized sufficiently for a workable emergency aid package to take effect. In the long term, it may be decades before the rural west Colombian economy fully recovers.

ALPS AUSTRIA
February 1999 AVALANCHE

Right: Avalanches like this one caused the deaths of nearly 86 tourists at the height of the Alpine ski season.

Before February 1999, the Alpine ski resorts of Austria, Switzerland, Italy, and France, had endured a succession of snow-starved seasons. So when heavy snowfalls arrived at the beginning of the month there was a general air of relief within the region's tourism industry. At last the foreign visitors would get the conditions they wanted. Tills would ring, hotels would fill, and the local economy would celebrate a much-needed boost. All seemed set for a memorable spring.

Memorable it was—but for entirely the wrong reasons. By the end of February a total of 86 skiers had died in weather-related incidents—half of them buried alive in two devastating avalanches which ripped through the Paznaun valley villages of Galtür and Valzur in Austria. Tour operators were soon busy organizing mass evacuations as parents from across Europe, anxious about risking their children's lives during half-term skiing holidays, demanded to be brought home. Other visitors were horrified to discover that they were stranded in areas accessible only by helicopter.

The season, which had promised so much had degenerated into chaos and tragedy.

The cause of the crisis lay not only in the heaviest snow for half a century—more than three and a half meters (11 feet) in the space of four weeks—but in a combination of unusual meteorological conditions. Two weather systems—the first in late January; the second in mid-February—produced fluctuating air temperatures. This in turn resulted in heavy, wet snow falling on top of lighter, dry snow, creating a highly unstable base. To complicate matters, winds of up to 145 kilometers per hour (90 miles per hour) were battering the mountains, leaving some slopes almost bare and others buried beneath massive accumulations. Under normal circumstances the authorities might have bombed high-risk areas to create controlled avalanches. But around Galtür, particularly, visibility was so bad that this strategy had to be ruled out. Meanwhile, frustrated skiers were cramped together in claustrophobic conditions that created their own social problems.

On February 17, blizzard conditions returned to Galtür and German tourists besieged the town hall chanting "Get Us Out!" Over the ensuing 48 hours several small avalanches were reported in the vicinity of the town, although the official line was that the slopes remained generally safe. By the 20th however, one experienced meteorologist, Erhard Berger, was emphasizing that avalanche warnings were in force for the entire area. Some tour operators responded by airlifting clients out of the resort but other companies continued to bring them in. Many holiday makers had either failed to recognize the degree of risk or were determined not to see their cherished ski vacation go to waste. Their package deals would not offer compensation for "acts of God," such as poor weather.

The disaster at Galtür might have been even worse had it not been for the efforts of local ski instructors to arrange entertainment for holiday makers unable to reach the slopes. They organized a traditional ski-race through the village streets and this ensured that many of the 3,000 or so visitors and 700 residents were gathered outside to watch. Even so, when at 4.00 pm an 800 meter (2,600 feet) section of snow directly above the village broke off and headed downhill at 210 kilometers per hour (130 miles per hour) there remained around 80 occupants in four buildings near the local church. Almost half never made it out alive despite the Herculean efforts of hopelessly under-equipped rescue workers.

Survivors spoke of how the "sky went black" as the white cloud struck. "The incredible thing was that there was absolutely no sound," said Chris Laming, a British skier. "All we saw was the light go out and this swirling powder snow crash into the hotel windows. It was absolutely terrifying. Parents were searching everywhere for their children.'

The aftermath of the disaster brought bitter recriminations as some skiers prepared to sue their package operators for failing to warn in advance of the treacherous conditions. One German woman threatened to bring charges of manslaughter against the Austrian tourism authorities, alleging that she had been "lied to and cheated" over the safety of the slopes. "I cannot accept," she later told reporters "that so many people have had to die—for profit."

OKLAHOMA USA
May 3, 1999 **TORNADO**

Although Oklahoma lies at the heart of "Tornado Alley," nothing prepared its citizens for the fury that was unleashed on the afternoon and evening of May 3, 1999. Not one, but a series of over 50 violent twisters ripped through the state and its neighbors, more than have ever been seen in a single day before. The first was spotted at about 5.00 pm near Cyril in south eastern Caddo County and, soon after, hail the size of baseballs was reported in Altus. By 5.40 pm reports were flooding into weather stations of tornadoes touching down all over the state, and they did not stop until after 11.00 pm. In their path the twisters left death and destruction on an unprecedented scale. After the ruins had been picked through and the missing accounted for, the death toll stood at 43, while 795 were seriously injured. In addition to the human carnage, the tornadoes destroyed homes and businesses, leaving the US government with a bill of 750 million dollars.

The aftermath saw scenes that would usually be associated with third world countries as people, carrying whatever they had managed to salvage, poured out of the cities, and neighborhoods, looking for somewhere to stay.

US Representative J.C. Watts, who visited the region the next day said of the tragedy, "If you didn't see it with your own eyes, you couldn't comprehend it. It's like someone piece-by-piece taking the houses apart and then just throwing them up in the air. They landed wherever—cars on top of houses, on top of rubble."

Above: This field shows the tracks made by huge bales of hay as one of the Oklahoma tornadoes swept them across the landscape.

CREDITS FOR NATURAL DISASTERS